NEBS
MANAGEMENT
DEVELOPMENT

SUPER SERIES

THIRD EDITION
Managing Activities

Understanding
Quality

Published for
&& NEBS Management *by*

Pergamon
Flexible
Learning

Pergamon Flexible Learning
An imprint of Butterworth-Heinemann
Linacre House, Jordan Hill, Oxford OX2 8DP
225 Wildwood Avenue, Woburn, MA 01801-2041
A division of Reed Educational and Professional Publishing Ltd

℞ A member of the Reed Elsevier plc group

OXFORD   AUCKLAND   BOSTON
JOHANNESBURG   MELBOURNE   NEW DELHI

First published 1986
Second edition 1991
Third edition 1997
Reprinted 1998, 1999, 2001 (twice)

British Library Cataloguing in Publication Data
A catalogue record for this book is available from the British Library

ISBN 0 7506 3296 8

For information on all Butterworth-Heinemann publications
visit our website at www.bh.com

FOR EVERY TITLE THAT WE PUBLISH, BUTTERWORTH-HEINEMANN
WILL PAY FOR BTCV TO PLANT AND CARE FOR A TREE.

The views expressed in this work are those
of the authors and do not necessarily reflect
those of the National Examining Board for
Supervision and Management or of the publisher.

NEBS Management Project Manager: Diana Thomas
Author: Joe Johnson
Editor: Fiona Carey
Series Editor: Diana Thomas
Based on previous material by: Joe Johnson
Composition by Genesis Typesetting, Rochester, Kent
Printed and bound in Great Britain

Contents

Workbook introduction

Here are the workbook titles in each module which link with *Understanding Quality*, should you wish to extend your study to other Super Series workbooks. There is a brief description of each workbook in the User Guide.

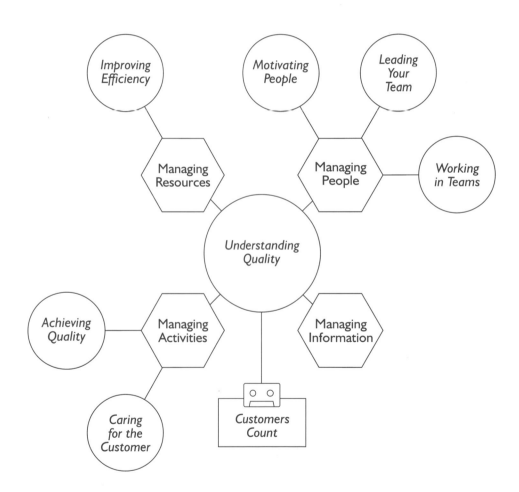

2 S/NVQ links

This workbook relates to the following elements:

A1.1   Maintain work activities to meet requirements
A1.2   Maintain healthy, safe and productive working conditions
A1.3   Make recommendations for improvements to work activities
F5.1   Provide advice and support for the assessment of processes and working environments
F5.2   Provide advice and support for the development of plans to improve quality systems

It is designed to help you to demonstrate the following Personal Competences:

- analysing and conceptualizing;
- building teams;
- focusing on results;
- thinking and taking decisions;
- striving for excellence.

3 Workbook objectives

'In general use, we tend to speak of high quality as being superior to low quality. In so doing, we imply that some attribute, such as designed life, has a higher value to us. A pair of shoes is, in these terms, of high quality if it gives five years' wear instead of two. Yet, what of the people who do not want shoes to last five years? To these customers, fitting the fashion may rank more highly than fitting the foot! In short, they prefer a different combination of attributes. Clearly, in any product, there are many. Customers search for those that most closely fit what they want.'

John Naylor (1995), *Operations Management*, Pitman.

This paragraph expresses the difficulty we encounter when trying to understand quality, for quality does not mean the same to everyone. At the same time, the last sentence contains a definition of quality. A good answer to the question 'What is quality?' is that **quality is whatever the customer wants it to mean**.

The customer comes first, second and third, so far as quality is concerned; this is one of the themes of this workbook.

There are three sessions. Session A deals with definitions, and looks at various aspects of the subject: design quality and process quality; quality systems; the benefits and the beneficiaries; costs; reliability; and accreditation against standards.

Session B is all about total quality management: what it is, and its main components, which are total commitment, a focus on the customer, continuous improvement and teamwork.

Then, in Session C, we try to find ways of applying the knowledge we've gained.

3.1 Objectives

When you have completed this workbook you will be **better able to**:

- explain what quality means;
- recognize the benefits of quality improvement and development in your work, and appreciate methods of establishing the costs of quality;
- have a good understanding of total quality management;
- identify your customers and find ways of improving the quality of the goods and services you provide them;
- lead your team in taking practical and positive steps towards higher work quality.

4 Activity planner

You may want to look at the following Activities now so that you can make prior arrangements:

Activity 19. Here you are being asked to give an example of a particular quality goal and how you set about achieving it;

Activity 20. Invites you to consider communication with your team;

Activity 21. Here you are being asked to give an example of a recommendation you have made, or intend to make, regarding improvements to quality.

Portfolio of evidence

Some or all of these Activities may provide the basis of evidence for your S/NVQ portfolio. All Portfolio Activities and the Work-based assignment are signposted with this icon.

The icon states the elements to which the Portfolio Activities and Work-based assignment relate.

The Work-based assignment asks you to identify your customers, find ways of plugging the gap between what they want and what you give them and make recommendations for improvements. This relates specifically to element A1.2 but will also help you meet elements D1.1 and D1.2 of the MCI Management Standards: 'Gather required information' and 'Inform and advise others.' You may want to prepare for it in advance.

Session A Quality and customers

1 Introduction

What is quality?

Is quality the same as excellence, and if so, how do we know when something is excellent? What makes one thing of higher quality than another? Why is quality important: what benefits does it bring? Should you expect to pay more for quality goods and services? What is ISO 9000?

By the time you have finished reading this session, the answers to these and other related questions should become clearer. We start by establishing definitions, because quality is one of those words which is much used and little understood.

Assuming we know what quality is, how can we ensure that we deliver it? To achieve this, any supplier organization has to find out, firstly, what the **customer** wants, so that goods or services can be designed to meet those wants. The organization's customer is the one who ultimately makes all the decisions about quality, and sets all the standards. That's an important lesson to learn: whenever we consider quality, our main focus has to be on the customer.

The second step for the supplier is to ensure that the product or service conforms with the agreed design. In addition, so as to ensure that the required level of quality is delivered to the customer, the organization has to set up a system of quality management, which includes quality assurance and quality control.

2 Defining quality

You may well already have your own views about quality: what it is and how to achieve it. Let's start by seeing how far we agree.

2.1 What quality is

'Quality' is something which is talked about a lot at work and more generally. But do we all mean the same thing when we use the term?

Activity 1

Define the word 'quality' in your own words. Think about your own job and organization as you answer this. What do you mean when you talk about 'quality' at work?

_____

_____

_____

There have been a number of definitions given of quality. If we look to some famous experts in the subject, we find that they define quality as:

- 'Meeting of customers' needs' (W. Edwards Deming);
- 'Fitness for use' (J.M. Juran);
- 'Conformance to requirements' (Philip B. Crosby).

Others textbook definitions include:

- 'meeting, or exceeding, customer requirements';
- 'the degree to which a product or service satisfies customers' requirements'.

Perhaps you worded your definition something along these lines, or said that quality means 'doing things right first time' or 'delivering goods or services of the highest standard'. You may even have quoted the words in the workbook introduction, and said that quality is whatever the customer wants it to mean.

As you would expect, there is an 'official' definition, given in British Standard 4778 (ISO 8402) 'Glossary of terms used in quality assurance':

Quality is: 'The totality of features and characteristics of a product or service that bear on its ability to satisfy stated or implied needs.'

This definition has been adopted internationally, and is also used, for example, by the American Society for Quality Control.

Activity 2

3 mins

Read the British Standard definition again and answer the following question:

Whose 'stated or implied needs' do you think are to be satisfied?

_____

_____

> The customer is not always the same as the 'user' or 'consumer'. For example, if you buy your dog a tin of pet food, you are the customer, and the dog is the consumer.

The simplest and best answer to this question is 'the customers' needs'. Customers are the people who buy or use the goods or services provided by an organization.

Every organization has customers. Where products or services are bought and sold, the customer makes the purchase, and is easily identified. In other kinds of organization, different words such as 'client', 'patient', 'tenant' or 'pupil' may be used instead of 'customer', but the result is the same. In general, the customer pays the bill, either directly or indirectly; and customers are the only reason that an organization exists.

In some situations, such as when patients require medical treatment, customers are not in a good position to know what they need. Normally, however, 'what the customer needs' does **not** mean 'what the organization thinks is good for the customer'; it means 'what the customer wants or expects'.

So we can say that

achieving quality means meeting the customers' wants or expectations.

This implies that organizations have mechanisms that can establish what the customer wants or expects, and whether or not the customer is getting it.

The customer is the focus of all discussions about quality.

(We mustn't forget that there are customers inside the organization, too. That's a topic we'll look at in the next session.)

But what does the customer want or expect? What do you, as a customer, want or expect when you buy something?

2.2 The dimensions of quality

Activity 3

If you go into a shop to buy something, say a new coat, which of the following would you think of as being to do with the quality of the article?

Relevant to quality?

■ The style. YES NO

■ The colour. YES NO

■ The way it is made. YES NO

■ The finish. YES NO

■ The fit. YES NO

■ The way you are treated in the shop. YES NO

■ How well you think the item is likely to wear. YES NO

■ The price. YES NO

■ How good it makes you feel. YES NO

■ The reputation of the shop. YES NO

■ The reputation of the manufacturer. YES NO

You would have been right to answer 'yes' to **all** of these, because they all have a bearing on your decision whether or not to purchase.

There are many aspects or dimensions of quality. One way to list them is as follows.

■ **Utility or performance**: the main characteristics of a product or service. This determines what a product does and how well it does it, or what a service provides, and how well it provides it. For example, the performance of a dry-cleaning service would be measured by how well clothes are cleaned.

- **Features**: the distinctive properties of products or services, which help to distinguish them from similar offerings. Features may be integral to the item, such as an automatic range finder on a camera, or may be secondary, such as being treated with respect and consideration if you are a patient.
- **Reliability**: the probability that the product will not fail within a certain period of time, or that a service will be of a consistently high standard. (We will look at the subject of reliability later in this session.) Reliability includes:

  - **Maintainability**: how easily and quickly a product can be repaired when it fails.
  - **Availability**: the degree to which a product or service is available when the user needs it.
  - **Durability**: how long a product will last before it has to be discarded.

- **Usability**: the safety, convenience and (perhaps) comfort of a product in use.
- **Serviceability**: the safety, convenience and (perhaps) duration of a service.
- **Price**: what the product or service costs. Customers do not always go for the lowest price, partly because the amount of money they spend affects their own self-image.
- **Conformance:** how well a product or service meets its specifications. If you buy a car which is described as having metallic paint and anti-lock brakes, that's what you expect to get.
- **Aesthetics**: what a product looks like, and how it feels, sounds, tastes, and smells. This dimension is probably the hardest to define, as it depends on customers' perceptions and perhaps on fashions and trends.

One other dimension of quality is **perceived quality**: what impression the customer has of the quality of the product or service, which may or may not be based on complete information.

Customers are often unable to find out everything they want to know before making a purchasing decision, and may not be able to form the right questions to ask. As customers, we would all like to know not only what features are available, but (for example) how reliable or available are the goods or services we buy. Advertisements do not always help, as they usually contain selective information – or none at all! Decisions frequently have to be made based on:

- assurances of sales staff;
- the 'image' that the maker's name conjures up;
- recommendations of friends or product reviewers;
- experiences of similar products or services.

It is useful to keep in mind the fact that all these dimensions of quality exist, and that the concept of quality is not one simple idea. It has many forms and aspects, as our definition of quality implies. To remind you:

Quality is: 'The totality of features and characteristics of a product or service that bear on its ability to satisfy stated or implied needs.'

Now let's look at a couple of further definitions.

5

3 Design quality and process quality

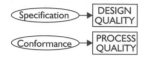

In order to satisfy customers' wants and expectations, a supplier or service provider must do two things:

1   determine what those wants and expectations are, and agree a specification for the product or service which will meet or exceed them;

2   ensure that the product or service conforms with the agreed specification.

The first step is the **design quality**; the second is **process quality**.

Design quality can be defined as the degree to which the specification of the product or service satisfies customers' wants and expectations.

Process quality is the degree to which the product or service, when it is transferred to the customer, conforms to specifications.

For example, a maker of television sets will survey the market, and try to find out what level of performance and which features customers want and expect, for the price they are prepared to pay. This will depend on the current technology, what features competitors are offering, and so on. The manufacturer will then set out a specification and design a television set to achieve this performance and these features. It will then need to ensure that every set it makes conforms to the specification.

A supermarket chain will go through a similar process, even though it may carry a vast range of products, and may not manufacture any of them. It has to determine what customers want, to specify the features and performance of these products, and to ensure that its suppliers consistently meet the specifications.

Sometimes, the delivery is the most important aspect. In the 'service' that a theatre provides, for instance, the audience's reaction will depend on how well the play is performed. But a high quality performance can only be achieved through the talents of both the production team and the players.

But let's pause for a moment, because, in listing our two steps of design quality and process quality, we have rather simplified the business of satisfying customers' wants.

Activity 4

3
mins

What factors have we ignored by summarizing quality development as: 'Find out what the customer wants, specify it, and then make sure the item meets the specification'? Jot down two factors.

_____

_____

_____

_____

_____

_____

A few of the aspects which make the whole business of achieving the right quality more complicated, are listed below. You may have mentioned others.

■ It can be very difficult to discover what the customer wants. As we have already discussed, the customer can't always be specific about particular wants and expectations.

■ Very often, until goods or services are put on offer by the supplier, the customer cannot know how desirable they are.

■ Performance and/or features are frequently driven by technology or fashion, rather than by customers directly.

■ The specification process is fraught with difficulties; for example, it may be hard to:

　■ describe a design in terms that allow it to be manufactured easily;
　■ define a level of service in such a way that staff know exactly what they have to do in order to achieve it.

However, every organization has to overcome the difficulties, and to develop products and services that customers will buy.

But how does an organization design goods or services to an agreed specification, and ensure conformance to that specification? It can only do this through a **system of quality management**.

4 Quality systems

EXTENSION I
This definition is given in the book listed on page 76.

A quality system has been defined by Dennis F. Kehoe as:

The organizational structure, responsibilities, procedures, processes and resources for implementing quality management.

The quality systems of an organization will determine how successful it is in achieving the required product and service quality. In the next session, we discuss total quality management. For the moment, however, let us focus on quality control and quality assurance, which, until fairly recently at least, have been the terms used for 'the work that the quality department does'. These are the systems that are set up mainly to ensure conformance to specification.

4.1 Quality control

Quality control (QC) is concerned with the operational techniques and activities that are used to fulfil requirements for quality.

Typically, quality control specialists will be involved in:

- inspection and testing of materials, parts, assemblies and final products, to see whether they conform to defined standards and specifications;
- using charts and basic statistics to check results and feed back data;
- maintaining and validating test equipment;
- sampling services to see whether they meet desired quality levels.

4.2 Quality assurance

Quality control is part of **quality assurance (QA)**.

Quality assurance is defined in BS 4778 as

'All those planned and systematic actions necessary to provide adequate confidence that a product or service will satisfy given requirements for quality.'

Quality assurance is intended to implement and manage a **quality system**. It may be involved in:

- producing and maintaining a **quality manual**, which defines the organization's quality system;
- ensuring conformance to the quality system;
- supplier approval;
- analysing statistical quality data;
- (perhaps) analysing quality costs;
- quality planning.

> Quality assurance is the system of documented controls within your business that ensures you never let a customer down.'
> — John Shaw in *BS EN ISO 9000 Made Simple*.

It has long been realized that simply checking the quality of products is not enough. The quality assurance system must take control of all stages of product manufacture, because:

effective quality must be based on prevention, not detection.

However, the idea of QA as a separate function **within** an organization is also now recognized as being outdated. Quality assurance must exist, but the **whole** organization must be involved in promoting and improving quality. This philosophy is embodied in a system called **total quality management (TQM)**, which we will discuss in the next session.

So TQM incorporates QA, and QA incorporates QC, as the following diagram suggests.

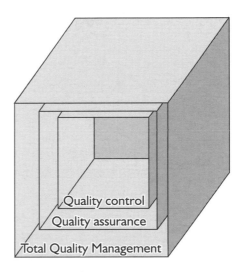

5 Why is quality important?

We have discussed the fact that product or service quality depends on both design quality and process quality. If we focus on an organization which is trying to improve the quality of its products, we can see that there are two parallel developments going on:

- **product improvements**, which are required to meet the changing wants and expectations of the customer, and
- **process improvements**, resulting from the desire to make production of goods or services more efficient and effective.

Activity 5

For any commercial company, what would you say was the driving force behind **both** these developments?

_____

There is a simple one-word answer to this question: **competition**. The following is a longer explanation.

5.1 Competition

The reason for trying to make better products and services available, and for trying to become more efficient and effective at producing them is that:

- commercial organizations are in business to make a profit,

  ⇨ - and they do this by selling goods and/or services;

- customers will only buy these goods or services if they meet their wants and expectations,

  ⇨ - so that the better the customers' wants and expectations are met, the more products and services can be sold;

- as more products and services are sold, profits will tend to rise,

  ⇨ - thus if products and services are produced more efficiently and effectively, costs will fall, and profits will rise.

On the other hand:

- if the customers' wants and expectations are not met sufficiently well, they will buy competitors' products and services instead;

  ⇨ - and if production is not efficient and effective, costs will be too high, and the company will fail.

5.2 Non-profit-making organizations

Perhaps you work for an organization that isn't expected to make a profit: a public service organization, for example. If you do, you might argue that your 'company' won't fail, because it doesn't compete with others, and your customers cannot choose to go elsewhere. 'In any case,' you may say, 'our income is assured, as it comes from public funds'.

In the short term, a non-profit-making organization may believe it doesn't need to worry too much about satisfying its customers. But this can never be true in the longer term. Organizations of all kinds come under scrutiny, and quality standards may be imposed as a result of external inspection. Customers can also apply pressure in a number of ways: through their votes in elections, via the media, by complaining to local members of parliament, and so on.

A school or a hospital cannot afford to continue providing a poor service, for it may ultimately be closed down if it does. A county council or a government that doesn't please its citizens will find itself voted out of office. Inefficient staff are likely to be replaced. In the past few years, whole sectors of public service have found themselves privatized: the telecommunications, gas, electricity and water industries are obvious examples. No organization can escape the demands of its customers for high quality.

And even organizations that don't have to make a profit do not have unlimited funds. Money must always be spent wisely, and in response to the needs of customers.

5.3 Consumer legislation

Here's another reason why quality is important.

Consumer protection legislation makes manufacturers and suppliers liable for any personal injury or damage of property suffered by someone using an unsafe or defective product.

Under the Consumer Protection Act 1987, it is not necessary to prove a manufacturer negligent for a claim to be made. Instead, the only issue at stake is whether the product was defective, and whether its state was the cause of the claimant's injuries. Thus one defective item could result in a lawsuit.

So a further reason why quality is important is that suppliers and manufacturers will want to ensure that every product that is shipped to a customer is safe. The quality system that must be set up to achieve high levels of quality consistently, is precisely that which will ensure the safety of every item. Such a system must:

■ keep products and services under careful control;
■ pay attention to every detail in product and process development.

5.4 Other beneficiaries

As we have discussed, the organization will benefit from quality improvements, because organizations providing the best quality are likely to achieve the highest sales, and to make the biggest profits. (To repeat: by high quality we do not mean expensive or luxury items; we mean goods that meet the customers' wants and expectations.)

They are also least likely to be made liable under the consumer protection laws.

But who else benefits from high quality?

Activity 6

3 mins

Apart from the supplying organization, which other groups of people would you expect to benefit from high quality products and services? Jot down two groups of people you think would benefit, and briefly explain your reasons.

_____

_____

_____

_____

_____

_____

You may have responded by listing:

- the **employees** of the organization, for at least two reasons. As the organization becomes more successful, so greater benefits and greater job security can be passed on to employees. Also, the morale in a successful, high quality organization is likely to be higher.
- the organization's **customers** (and users), because they will receive goods and services of the quality they want.

As we will discuss in the next session, the concept of internal customers embraces the idea that these two groups can turn out to be the same.

Now we turn from benefits to costs.

6 The cost of quality

Few organizations know how much they spend on quality. According to Crosby:

'In manufacturing the price is typically 25 per cent or more of revenue; service companies spend 40 per cent or more of operating expenses.'

However, there are two important statements to make with regard to costs.

The first was expressed in the title of Philip Crosby's original best-seller, *Quality is Free*. The message was that:

'Quality is measured by the price of nonconformance.'

In other words:

the cost of achieving competitive levels of quality is lower than the cost of not achieving them.

The second important point to recognize is that the best managed organizations have been able to reduce their costs of quality to as little as 3 per cent of sales, over a period of time. And they have done this while improving the quality of the product.

Let's look first at how costs can be assessed.

6.1 The cost components

What are the costs of quality?

Activity 7

3 mins

Think about your own organization, and the broad areas where money is spent on achieving high quality. You might start by imagining that your team or your organization delivered very poor products or services. What costs would be incurred as a result?

_____

_____

_____

Now assume you wanted to set about improving things. How would this result in extra costs?

_____

_____

_____

Would you expect overall costs to be higher when quality was very poor, or when it was very good? (Explain your reasoning.)

_____

_____

_____

_____

_____

You may have said that:

- poor quality would lead to lots of complaints, and that it would be an expensive business trying to keep customers happy in this situation;
- trying to improve quality will cost a great deal in training, checking and inspection, finding better suppliers, and so on;
- it would be difficult to compare costs between the situations of poor and high quality, but that continued poor quality wasn't really an option.

If we analyse quality costs, we find they can be separated into four components:

- prevention costs;
- appraisal costs;
- internal failure costs;
- external failure costs.

There is more than one way of assessing quality costs, and the two main approaches are described in British Standard BS 6143. Its two parts are:

BS 6143 Part 1: 1992 *Process Cost Model*

BS 6143 Part 2: 1990 *Prevention, Appraisal and Failure Model.*

We will only discuss the latter.

They are grouped as shown in the next figure:

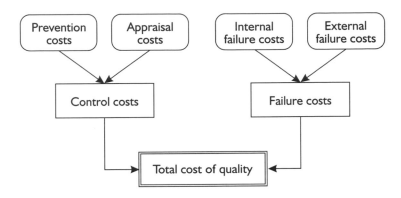

Defective goods and services must be eliminated before they reach the customer, and this can be done either through prevention or appraisal.

These are the **control** costs.

Prevention costs include:

- **identifying what customers want**;
- **producing specifications**, plans, manuals and procedures;
- organizing a **quality assurance** system;
- **assessing suppliers**;
- **training**.

Appraisal costs include:

- determining the quality of **incoming goods** and services;
- **inspecting and testing** of goods and services to ensure product or process conformance.

Failures may occur either internally (during the production process), or externally (after the product or service has been delivered).

These are the **failure** costs.

Internal failure costs include the costs of:

- producing items that then have to be **reworked, scrapped, or sold at a reduced price**, or providing services that the customer considers **ineffective** or **inadequate**;
- **investigating** reasons for failure;
- **idle facilities and people** as a result of failures.

External failure costs include the costs of:

- **making refunds**, and repairing or replacing items, during the warranty period;
- handling **customer complaints**;
- **recalling products**, if they are found to be dangerous, for example;
- **losing customers** through their being dissatisfied.

When organizations do consider the cost of quality, they may be misled into believing that there is a trade-off to be made between costs and quality.

6.2 Quality costs – the traditional view

According to the traditional view of quality costs, there is a 'law of diminishing returns'. Look at the graph below, which is intended to support this view.

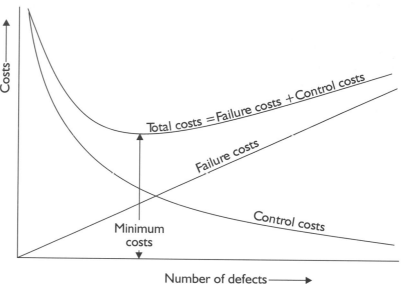

The theory is that:

'Failure costs keep going up, in direct proportion to the number of defects. So you must invest in controlling your quality. The problem is that, if you want to get your quality up to a very high level (that is, to the left of the graph), you have to invest an enormous amount. As total costs are the sum of failure costs and control costs, and the best compromise is to aim for a point where these total costs are a minimum.'

Activity 8

3 mins

It sounds convincing enough, but what are the implications? Can you see any flaws in this traditional argument?

_____

_____

_____

_____

_____

_____

Perhaps you agree with this view, which says we should not aim to reach the fewest number of failures, but should invest just enough in controlling quality to minimize the total costs. This implies that, for the supplier, there is an 'acceptable' failure rate:

- the manufacturer will be satisfied to always allow a certain number of defects to slip through;
- the service provider will plan to allow a certain amount of inefficiency.

But what about the customer?

Are you, as a customer, happy to accept that a few things will be wrong when, say, you take delivery of a new radio or washing machine? Or, if you go to hospital for an operation, and are told: 'We try not to make mistakes, but we can't afford to be so efficient that we don't lose a few patients', will you smile philosophically? If you're anything like the average customer, you'd be rather upset at such an attitude. In fact, if you have any choice, you'll go elsewhere for your goods and services.

So this traditional argument no longer stands up to reality: customers are increasingly reluctant to put up with shoddy goods or services. If you make compromises on quality, at the very least you can expect a lot of complaints. And if you ignore what your customers are telling you, **you won't survive**.

Many organizations nowadays no longer think along traditional lines, as the following story illustrates.

A European company ordered some components from a Japanese firm. The order stated: '10,000 items required, with a defect rate of 0.03%'. What they meant was that there should be no more than three defective items in the batch of 10,000. When the parts arrived, there were two boxes, one containing 9,997 good components, and another containing three defective ones, clearly labelled as such. The supplier could not understand why the customer wanted defective components, but it was happy to oblige.

Manufacturers are used to talking about 'acceptable quality levels (AQL)', a term that applies to statistical sampling. To explain: if you take a small sample from a large batch, the number of defective items in the sample will give you an idea of the total number there are likely to be in the batch. The AQL is the maximum percentage of defectives in a sample, that can be considered acceptable as a process average. Unfortunately, the term 'acceptable quality level' is frequently interpreted to mean that it's OK to make defective goods.

AQL is only mentioned in passing here. It is dealt with more fully in the workbook *Achieving Quality*.

Philip Crosby, in his book *Quality is Still Free*, gives an insight into this attitude:

'When I started in the quality world in 1952 my first lesson was about AQLs. There was scientific proof that it cost a lot less to plan on things not being correct. "It would take a fortune to do everything right every time" was contained in every explanation. So all processes were planned around these statistics. It was a great performance standard because we weren't expected to do it right and when we didn't there was no problem. Suppliers had AQLs included in the purchase order so they could have a defect rate of 1 per cent, 2 per cent, and such. Sloppy executives love AQLs.

It was the frustration created by this belief that led me to create the Zero Defects concept in 1961. Suppliers would come to me, as quality manager of the weapons system project, for their "AQL". .... Software development for instance, wanted to know how many errors they could have per line of programming. ... My response was that they had bid the contract to supply this service or product and I expected it to appear exactly as promised. There would be no AQL.'

6.3 Adopting a better approach

The traditional approach to quality costs is flawed because it is based on the assumption that quality is achieved through quality control and inspection. It is certainly true that quality costs will be enormous if you have to rely on having someone to check everything at every stage. But many organizations have shown that, if you set up systems, and train people, so that mistakes are minimized, then costs can actually go down. This can be achieved through TQM.

So the graph we saw earlier doesn't tell the whole story. In the next graph, the original 'total costs' curve is shown at the top. Now, if we want to reduce costs *and* improve quality, we have to push the 'dip' in this curve downwards and to the left. This is exactly what happens as a result of TQM, as you can see.

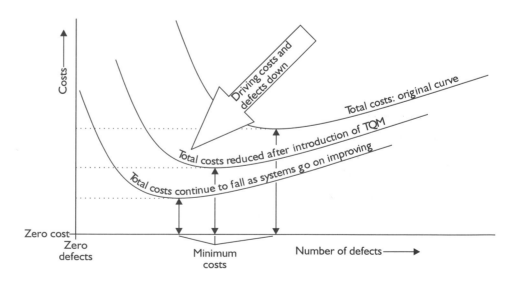

In summary,

the old idea of 'not spending too much on quality because you won't get your money back' is outdated, incorrect and is a recipe for failure.

7 Reliability

As mentioned earlier, an important aspect or dimension of quality is reliability.

Activity 9

Jot down in your own words what you understand when you hear a product or a service described as being reliable.

_____

_____

_____

If a person is reliable, you know you can depend on them – they won't let you down. When it comes to things, a good simple definition would be that if something is reliable, it will work when you need it.

Another, more precise definition of reliability is given in BS 4778 as:

'The ability of an item to perform a required function under stated conditions for a stated period of time.'

In relation to a service, the term is just as applicable. For example, if you visit the hairdresser regularly, you want to know that you can rely on getting your hair trimmed (or washed, or 'permed' or whatever), efficiently and to your liking, time after time.

7.1 The bath-tub curve

Most manufactured products have something in common with living creatures – they have a limited life-span.

The life-span of a product, like that of a living creature, can be separated into three time periods: infancy, working life, and 'old age'.

When we talk about the reliability of products, we generally refer to these time periods or regions as

- **Burn-in**: this name reflects the fact that many products are run in or 'burned in' immediately after they are produced;
- **Useful life**: the time when the product is in active use;
- **Wear-out**: the period when useful life has come to an end.

19

Look at the diagram below. It is a graph of the probability of failure rates for a number of products over their whole life-span.

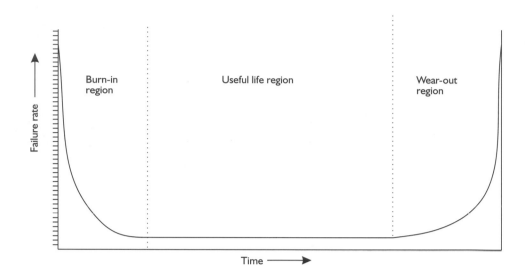

This is the typical **bath-tub curve** of reliability: the graph gets its name from its shape. You can see that the probability of failure drops during the burn-in period, and then is very low for a long time during the useful life region. Towards the end of its life, the probability of failure of the product rises once more. This is what you might expect.

- In 'infancy' there is more likelihood that the product will fail. There may have been faulty components or materials installed, or the product may have been incorrectly manufactured.
- As time goes by, all the faulty components and materials 'settle down' (or have been replaced). During the useful life of the product fewer failures can be expected.
- Later, components and materials start to wear out, and the rate of failure increases again.

Activity 10

4
mins

Do you think that services also tend to follow this 'bath-tub' curve? Do services 'burn-in' or 'wear out'? Briefly jot down your ideas on this subject. If you work in a service industry, try to imagine what kind of reliability curve would be applicable, if any.

_____

_____

_____

_____

_____

Let's think of an example. Suppose a local authority decides to set up a service to collect paper or other materials for recycling. It would perhaps need to let householders and firms know about the service, to distribute special containers, train staff, and so on. There would be many things to organize, and lots that might go wrong to start with: the authority could be overwhelmed (or 'under-whelmed') by the response, say, or it might find that people were still mixing up their rubbish with the paper. So we can say that there would be a period of settling down – equivalent to the 'burning in' of products.

After the initial period, when things are going smoothly, we would expect the problem rate to be low.

Like a product, which can fail at any time, a service can cease suddenly, by being withdrawn. In the case of the paper collection, a new council might decide it could no longer afford to provide this service. Services don't wear out, but they may change. For instance, the patients of a surgery might be unhappy if a doctor leaves and a new one arrives; they may experience a new settling-in period, as patients and doctor get to know one another.

There are products, too, which don't wear out. The words in a book, for example, will last indefinitely. The book itself may get damaged, or the printing ink may fade, but it's possible to make any number of copies of the original, and so preserve the writing for as long as we want to.

Another good example is computer software. As software consists only of programs and data, there is nothing to wear out. (On the other hand, software tends to have a very long 'burn-in' period before all the 'bugs' or design faults have been removed!)

Other kinds of products tend not to have a long flat part of the curve at all. A complex mechanical system will tend to wear out more quickly and more frequently than, say, an electrical one. The bath-tub curve for mechanical systems typically looks like the one shown below.

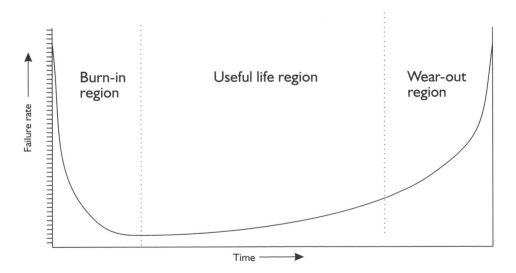

7.2 Reducing failure rates

Obviously, if you buy a product – a car, say – reliability is very important to you. But reliability is also important for the manufacturer of the product. Most manufacturers (and others who pass on the product, such as distributors) are likely to be very concerned about reliability. Similarly, service providers know that they will only continue to keep their customers by offering a reliable service.

As we've said, reliability is an aspect of quality. If products or services are unreliable, they don't provide the quality that customers demand. This will result in customers buying different products or services, or buying from competitors.

Activity 11

4 mins

How can a product or a service be made more reliable? Imagine you are responsible for the manufacture of an item of kitchen equipment, say, or for providing a school catering service. Knowing what you do about the way products and services fail, and thinking about the shape of the bath-tub curve, write down one action you might take to improve reliability.

_____

_____

_____

_____

_____

EXTENSION 1
If you would like to learn more about the important subject of reliability, the book *The Fundamentals of Quality Management*, by Dennis F. Kehoe, is recommended. This book devotes a whole chapter to reliability management.

There are a number of ways of trying to achieve high reliability.

■ If you think back to the bath-tub curve, you'll recall that failure rates are typically high during the 'infancy' of the product or service, shortly after it has been manufactured or set up. Obviously, it is important that customers are not involved until the 'flat' part of the curve has been reached. This means that the service or product must be adequately checked and run in, or tried out, **before** it is delivered.

■ Once a product is in use, or a service is running, the aim is (or should be) for there to be as few failures as possible. The supplier therefore needs to know how reliable its service or product is in normal use and how to make it more reliable.

Any organization concerned about reliability will study:

- how and why failures can occur, and
- what the consequences of each failure might be,

before it considers a product or service ready for the market.

What are the likely consequences of a failure? The most serious possible consequence, as we discussed earlier, is that someone is hurt. **Health and safety** is therefore a primary concern. Another is that one component in a product breaking down or being mishandled might cause other components to fail. It is for these reasons that designers aim to make their products 'fail safe'. For example, if a switch on a powered lawn-mower breaks, it should result in the power being kept off, not left on. Similarly, a user shouldn't be able to cause damage to a radio, say, by inserting the batteries the wrong way round.

A failure of a service might also result in a health or safety problem, and you could no doubt think of many obvious examples in medicine. Also, like products, services usually involve many groups or 'service components' acting independently, yet relying on one another. To get fresh fruit or vegetables half way round the world, and always in your local shop when you want to buy them, requires a great deal of coordination and organization, for example.

So we can say that the reliability of goods and services is a complex subject. High levels of reliability, like other aspects of quality, can only be achieved through careful planning.

That concludes our brief treatment of reliability. We switch subjects now, and look at quality standards and accreditation.

8 Certification and accreditation schemes

Over the past few years there has been growing pressure on manufacturers and service providers to comply with defined national and international standards, both for their products and for their quality systems. Let's start by looking at some important organizations.

8.1 The standards bodies

The main standards-setting body in this country is the **British Standards Institution (BSI)**. In fact, it was the first national standards body in the world. There are now more than 80 similar organizations in other countries. BSI publishes many thousands of standards and other publications, covering items as diverse as dentistry, computer languages and library buildings.

There are several international bodies which attempt to ensure that national standards are equivalent to one another. The most important of these is the **International Standards Organization (ISO)**.

One of the main aims of the **European Union (EU)** has been agreement on product quality standards. The intention is that goods which conform to the national standards of one member state will be accepted in all the other states.

At the end of 1992, the 'single market' was formed within the EU. Since this date:

■ only 'essential requirements' which relate to health, safety, consumer protection and the environment are the subject of agreement as EU standards. These are issued as 'Directives', and have the backing of the law.
■ except for these essential requirements, all member states have to recognize and accept test results and certificates issued by other EU national standards bodies.

8.2 Quality systems standards

However, we must distinguish between standards which define the required quality of products and services, and those standards which relate to **quality systems**. Quality systems standards set out the minimum requirements for an organization's quality assurance system. They are typically used:

■ to provide guidance to supplier organizations which are introducing quality assurance systems;
■ as a framework for evaluating the quality systems of suppliers;
■ to form the basis of a contract for quality system requirements.

Quality system standards should not be confused with product or service standards. They do not specify what a specific item is or does; instead they are intended to ensure that agreed levels of quality are met for any product or service.

Some system standards are related to a particular industry. The defence industry has used quality standards for many years. Examples of defence industry standards are:

■ AQAP 1–3 NATO Requirements for an Industrial Quality Control System;
■ AQAP 4–2 NATO Inspection System Requirements for Industry;
■ AQAP 9–2 NATO Basic Inspection Requirements for Industry.

Some large organizations have developed their own standards. The Ford Motor Company's Q101 Worldwide Supplier Quality System Standard is one example.

The most widely adopted **general** quality system standard is ISO 9000.

8.3 BS EN ISO 9000

BS EN ISO 9000 (as it is now known in this country) began life in 1979 as BS 5750, when it was introduced by the British Standards Institution. Since that time, the standard has been widely adopted in Britain, and conformance to this standard has long been a requirement of all government contracts.

BS 5750 was reissued, in slightly modified form, as ISO 9000, by the International Standards Organization, and this is used in countries throughout the world.

The full title of ISO 9000 is BS EN ISO 9000, and our comments can also be applied to BS 5750.

ISO 9000 is subdivided into three separate standards:

> **EXTENSION 5**
> On page 77 you can see a list of the elements which are included in the three standards.

- Level 1 (**ISO 9001** or BS 5750 Part 1) is intended for organizations that are involved in design, development, production, installation and servicing. It is particularly relevant where there is a design element to the product or service supplied. Manufacturing companies would require accreditation to ISO 9001, as would companies designing houses, pipelines, computer systems, financial systems, and so on.
- Level 2 (**ISO 9002** or BS 5750 Part 2) is applicable to organizations involved in production, installation and servicing, but where there is no design element. Because it is relevant to most organizations who supply goods or services, ISO 9002 is the most widely adopted standard.
- Level 3 (**ISO 9003** or BS 5750 Part 3) applies where conformance to specified requirements can be established adequately by inspection and testing the finished product or service. It is the least used standard.

8.4 The benefits of accreditation

Becoming accredited requires quite an investment of effort. Is it worth it?

Activity 12

3 mins

What do you think would be the benefits to an organization of accreditation to ISO 9000? Try to list **two** benefits. (If your own organization already has accreditation, you may find this question fairly easy.)

_____

_____

_____

_____

_____

There are several possible benefits, not the least of which is an increase in business. The following diagram gives an indication of how much companies have benefited from accreditation:

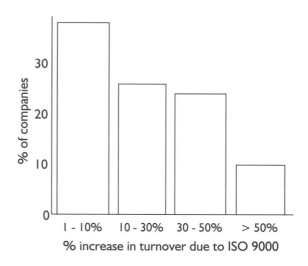

Other benefits are that:

- because the standard is so widely recognized, there is usually no need for an organization's quality system to undergo investigation by any customer, to any other standard, once accreditation to ISO 9000 has been achieved;
- buying from accredited suppliers gives the customer an assurance that the required level of quality of product or service will be reached – this is particularly important in view of the implications of consumer protection law;
- ISO 9000 provides a foundation upon which to build future quality improvements;
- many larger customers demand ISO 9000 accreditation of suppliers before they will award contracts.

8.5 But is ISO 9000 wholly beneficial?

Accreditation to ISO 9000 can certainly be beneficial to an organization, but the standard, and quality system standards generally, have their critics.

For one thing, there is a danger of assuming that quality can be achieved by following a set of rules. Philip Crosby points out in his book *Quality is Still Free* that:

'Governments, and associations, have the illusion that they can "assure quality" by imposing a specification such as ISO 9000 ... which is supposed to contain all the information and actions necessary to produce quality. This is the ultimate in naiveté. No-one would accept something similar for finance, marketing, administration, or any other function.'

EXTENSION 2
The book *Quality is Still Free* is full of useful and interesting ideas. Read it if you have time. It is listed on page 76.

Another 'quality guru' who has also been a critic of ISO 9000 is Joseph M. Juran. He has expressed the view that quality system standards do not deliver continuous quality improvement, or ensure world-class manufacturing performance.

Nevertheless, it has to be said that, especially for most smaller organizations, the introduction of the disciplines that are required for accreditation can bring about remarkable improvements. Perhaps the greatest danger is in assuming that, once this big step has been taken, there's nothing more to be done.

In Session C, we'll look at the steps to be taken in preparation for ISO 9000 implementation.

8.6 The IIP award

The **Investors in People (IIP)** award is often seen as being complementary to ISO 9000. It focuses on the management of people, and the contribution that this management makes both to the overall business mission and strategy, and to delivering high quality. Recruitment, development of staff and communications are among those aspects covered. Because IIP highlights the **people** in the organization, it is regarded as a way of humanizing the concentration on **systems** in ISO 9000.

Self-assessment I

20 mins

1   Give a valid definition of quality.

_____

_____

_____

_____

2   Match each of the following terms on the left with the correct description on the right.

Quality assurance (QA)	What a product looks like, and how it feels, sounds, tastes, and smells.
Process quality	The degree to which the specification of the product or service satisfies customers' wants and expectations.
Reliability	The degree to which the product or service, when it is transferred to the customer, conforms to specifications.
Design quality	All those planned and systematic actions necessary to provide adequate confidence that a product or service will satisfy given requirements for quality.
Aesthetics	This is concerned with the operational techniques and activities that are used to fulfil requirements for quality.
Quality control (QC)	The ability of an item to perform a required function under stated conditions for a stated period of time.

3   Identify the three regions in the diagram below.

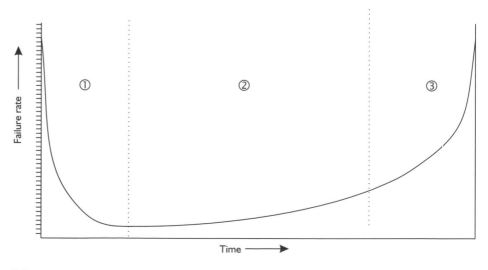

28

4   Fill in the correct terms in the table below:

P _____ costs
A _____ costs
} Control costs

I _____ costs
E _____ costs
} Failure costs

} T _____ _____ costs

5   Fill in the blanks in the following sentences with suitable words, chosen from the list below.

a   The main driving force behind quality is _____ .

b   The _____ is the focus of all discussions about quality.

c   _____ quality can be defined as the degree to which the _____ of the product or service satisfies customers' wants and expectations.

d   _____ quality is the _____ to which the product or service, when it is transferred to the customer, conforms to specifications.

e   A quality _____ can be defined as the organizational _____ , responsibilities, _____ , processes and resources for implementing quality management.

f   Quality is measured by the price of _____ .

g   Reliability is the _____ of an item to perform a required _____ under stated conditions for a stated period of time.

ABILITY	COMPETITION	CUSTOMER	DEGREE
DESIGN	FUNCTION	NONCONFORMANCE	PROCEDURES
PROCESS	SPECIFICATION	STRUCTURE	SYSTEM

Answers to these questions can be found on pages 79–80.

9 Summary

- BS 4778 (ISO 8402) defines quality as **'The totality of features and characteristics of a product or service that bear on its ability to satisfy stated or implied needs.'**

- Put more simply, we can say that achieving **quality means meeting the customers' wants or expectations**, because:

  - **the customer is the focus of all discussions about quality**.
  - The **dimensions of quality** include: **utility or performance**; **features**; **reliability**; **usability**; **serviceability**; **price**; **conformance**; **aesthetics**.

- A further dimension of quality is **perceived quality**: what impression the customer has of the quality of the product or service.

- **Design quality** and **process quality** are both integral parts of quality development. Design quality can be defined as the degree to which the specification of the product or service satisfies customers' wants and expectations. Process quality is the degree to which the product or service, when it is transferred to the customer, conforms to specifications.

- **Quality control (QC)** is concerned with the operational techniques and activities that are used to fulfil requirements for quality.

- **Quality assurance (QA)** is defined in BS 4778 as **'All those planned and systematic actions necessary to provide adequate confidence that a product or service will satisfy given requirements for quality'**.

- QA incorporates QC, and TQM (**Total Quality Management**) incorporates QA. It is a serious mistake to think that quality assurance is the business of one group or department.

- The main driving force behind quality is competition. Non-competitive organizations usually have other pressures acting upon them to drive up quality.

- Organizations, customers and employees all benefit from quality.

- In the PAF (prevention, appraisal and failure) model of quality costing, **prevention costs** and **appraisal costs** comprise **control costs**; internal and external **failure costs**, together with control costs comprise **total quality costs**.

- In theory, high levels of quality 'cost a fortune', but this assumes quality is achieved through appraisal, rather than prevention. Also, it does not take into account the fact that standards are going up, and that customers are much less ready to accept defective products or inadequate services. Thus the old idea of 'not spending too much on quality because you won't get your money back' is outdated, incorrect and a recipe for failure.

- **Reliability** is 'The ability of an item to perform a required function under stated conditions for a stated period of time.'

- The **'bath-tub'** curve reflects the fact that product failures are typically high during 'infancy' and 'old age'. Modified forms of the curve apply to products and services of all kinds.

- The **British Standards Institution** was the first standards body in the world. The most important international body is the **International Standards Organization (ISO)**.

- The most widely adopted general **quality system** standard is **ISO 9000.** It is subdivided into:

  - Level 1 (**ISO 9001** or BS 5750 Part 1) for organizations that are involved in design, development, production, installation and servicing.
  - Level 2 (**ISO 9002** or BS 5750 Part 2), applicable to organizations involved in production, installation and servicing, but where there is no design element.
  - Level 3 (**ISO 9003** or BS 5750 Part 3) applies where conformance to specified requirements can be established adequately by inspection and testing the finished product or service.

- Benefits of accreditation to ISO 9000 include:

  - the likelihood of increased business;
  - use as a foundation on which to build future quality programmes.

- ISO 9000, and quality system standards generally, have their critics. Perhaps the greatest danger is in assuming that, once this big step has been taken, there's nothing more to be done.

- The **Investors in People (IIP)** award is often seen as being complementary to ISO 9000. It focuses on the management of people, and the contribution that this management makes to the overall business mission and strategy, and to delivering high quality.

Session B Towards total quality

1 Introduction

'In quality management these are the Absolutes: Quality means conformance to requirements; Quality is obtained through prevention; Quality has a performance standard of zero defects; Quality is measured by the price of nonconformance.'

– Philip B. Crosby, *Quality is Still Free.*

'In the future there will be two kinds of company – those who have implemented Total Quality and those who have gone out of business. You do not have to do this – survival is not compulsory.'

– Dr Edwards Deming.

EXTENSION 1
The many aspects of total quality management are discussed at length in the book *The Fundamentals of Quality Management* by Dennis F. Kehoe.

During the last decade or so, many organizations have begun to adopt a new approach to quality management. This new approach is a result of the increasing emphasis on the importance of quality in products and services. It is now being realized that:

■ it is not enough to verify that products comply with requirements (inspection and quality control);
■ neither is it enough to install adequate quality systems to ensure that products are made to requirements (quality assurance).

If an organization wants to ensure the quality of its products, it has to **ensure the quality of all the designs and processes** that are used to make those products. This means that every person and every activity in an organization becomes involved in quality.

It is this exciting new perspective on quality that we look at in this session of the workbook.

2 The traditional approach to quality management

Until quite recently – the last ten or fifteen years – the management of a typical organization's quality system was assigned to one department and one manager. The quality assurance manager was held to be responsible for the quality of all goods and services. A commonly held view was that quality was something you 'added on' or 'inspected into' the organization's products, and that it was the quality manager's job to see that this was done.

While the chief executives of many companies would spend hours discussing finance or marketing, which they saw as being key to the organization's success, quality was largely ignored until customers complained about it. And when this happened, the quality manager would be chastised, and told to 'sort out the problem'. Philip Crosby says in his book *Quality is Still Free*:

'... as I learned more about managing quality, I realized that the conventional approach was not effective. Quality managers proudly stood up and announced that they personally were responsible for quality in a particular operation. Just as regularly, and not so proudly, they were sent down in flames when they were unable to resolve all the "quality problems" of the company.

As a project quality manager, I was berated each week by the program director in his staff meeting for not meeting desired goals while the real culprits from engineering, manufacturing, and sales hid their yawns and wished the whole thing would go away so they could return to their important work.

Crosby and many others were appalled by these traditional methods and attitudes, not least because they promoted a system that plainly didn't work very well. As we have already discussed, getting the quality right is the only way for a company to be successful. And to do that, a whole new approach is required.

Quality management has to:

■ be led from the top;
■ involve everyone in the organization;
■ be recognized as being vitally important.

This 'new thinking' has led to total quality management.

3 What is total quality management?

We mentioned the term **total quality management (TQM)** in the last session, and you may well have heard it talked about. But what is it?

Like other aspects of quality, TQM is, to some extent, open to interpretation. It has been described as a philosophy of quality that links policy and operational practice.

Some people would say that TQM is more than a philosophy: it is a way of life.

From another point of view, total quality management is a natural extension and development of quality systems – quality assurance and quality control – to cover all aspects, areas and people of an organization.

The three words 'total quality management' can be said to represent three elements. TQM:

- must be **total**, because it requires complete and unqualified **commitment** on behalf of everybody in the organization;
- is all about **quality**, which, as we agreed in our definition, means meeting the wants and expectations of customers;
- involves **management**, led from the top.

Key concepts, central to TQM are:

- **continuous improvement**;
- **teamwork**, involving **trust** and **empowerment**;
- **focusing on the customers' wants and expectations**.

(In case you have not come across the term 'empowerment' before, we will discuss it in Session C.)

A good definition of TQM would therefore be as follows.

Total quality management involves every member of the organization in a process of continuous improvement with the aim of satisfying the customers' wants and expectations.

Activity 13

4
mins

We have discussed reasons why an organization should be totally committed to quality. But not everyone agrees: some people think that the idea of TQM has been oversold. Write down what you think their main argument would be.

_____

_____

_____

_____

_____

You may put up the argument used by one company executive when attending a lecture on TQM:

'Why all this fuss about quality? Business is about survival – it's a competitive world. As a company, we can't afford to set ourselves ideals – we have to work to realities. Our quality is no worse than anyone else's. In any case, customers don't expect miracles – they want a reasonable package for a reasonable price.'

A response to this would be to say something like:

'It is certainly a competitive world. Competition is the main driving force behind quality. But an organization needs to be **better** than the competition. To do that it has to go on improving – or else get left behind. And to do that an organization needs total commitment.'

Another response is that customers are becoming more sophisticated and are tending to expect more for their money. They want that 'extra something', and if they think they can get it they will become dissatisfied with anything less. In fact, it has been said that

customers want more than to be satisfied – they want to be delighted!

To 'delight' customers, they have to be given **more** than they expect.

Another argument against TQM goes something like:

'Quality is not a philosophy, it's about giving the customers what they want. That means that you have to check everything carefully. Getting quality right is attention to detail, not high-flown theories.'

'Quality does not come about as the result of some particular way of dancing'.
– Philip Crosby.

Many would agree with this. Getting quality right is certainly all about attention to detail, as we will shortly discuss. And there's no harm in being sceptical about any theory if you find it unconvincing.

Now let's look at some of the aspects of the TQM model.

4 Continuous improvement

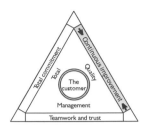

'... advocates of improvement, or kaizen, see striving for quality as an endless journey rather than a trip to a known and fixed destination.'
— John Naylor (1995), *Operations Management*, Pitman.

Continuous improvement is often referred to by its Japanese name, *kaizen*. It is characterized by:

- a large number of **detailed** improvements,
- over **a long period** of time,
- involving **teams** throughout the organization.

The accumulation of these small increments brings about large-scale advantages to the organization.

According to the philosophy of *kaizen*, everyone has two parts to his or her job:

- continuation: following current standards and practice;
- improvement: searching for higher standards and better ways of doing the work.

Examples of individual improvements are:

- reducing the amount of waste when cutting out patterns;
- taking less time to set up a machine;
- eliminating an unnecessary form to reduce time and effort spent on administration;
- finding an improved method of marking prices on goods.

'The people in TQM organizations have two jobs: job number one is the work they do; job number two is finding ways of improving job number one.' — Dennis F. Kehoe in *The Fundamentals of Quality Management* (see Extension 1).

The attention is on the **detail**. Continuous improvement is **not** simply a vague notion implying good intentions: it is about achieving real and lasting improvements at every stage. This can only be done through hard work, as Philip Crosby says in his book *Quality is Still Free*:

'People get angelic looks on their faces when they talk about continuous improvement. There are actually two different concepts involved. First is the popular one that says it is okay to drop six babies this week as long as we only plan to drop five next week. The second is that once we learn how to do things right, we are going to learn to get better all the time. Very few like the second. It is a lot of work.

37

5 Focus on the customer

It has been said that the best way to recognize a total quality organization is to watch how it deals with its customers.

We've all had experience of **poor** quality products and services. You go into a shop, ready to spend your money, and the shop assistants ignore you. You take your car to a garage to get it repaired, and after you've paid the bill are annoyed to find that the car still has the fault. You buy an expensive item of furniture and discover that the quality of finish is pretty dreadful. Or you stand in a queue for half an hour, only to find yourself face to face with a sour-faced and unhelpful counter clerk.

Activity 14

Describe how you feel when you are on the receiving end of poor quality products or services. (Just one sentence will do!)

_____

_____

Now say how you are likely to act when you experience excellent quality – when you find yourself delighted by the services or goods you buy.

_____

_____

_____

It may be that you felt you could sum up your feelings about poor quality in one word – 'terrible!' perhaps. You may also agree that when they buy inferior quality products, or receive bad service, most people tend to react by going somewhere else in future. It is estimated that up to 96 per cent of unhappy customers do not complain to the supplier, but these same people are very likely to convey their bad experiences to other potential customers.

What about the opposite kind of experience? If you are actually delighted by the quality of your purchase, you are surely much more inclined to go back to the same supplier for your next purchase.

Successful commercial organizations recognize that building up **customer loyalty** has to be a key element in their marketing strategy. How can this be done? Some of the ways are in:

- delivering a level of quality that is consistently high;
- putting the wants and expectations of the customer first – for without customers there is no business;
- establishing a culture in which all employees are expected to display a commitment to the customer.

5.1 Quality and internal customers

You may not work in direct contact with the **organization's** customers – the people who buy the products.

But **everybody** in the organization has a customer. Whoever is the next person or group to benefit from the work you do is your customer.

For example:

- the customers of the office cleaner are the people who work in the office;
- the customers of a team making printed circuits are the team whose job it is to place those printed circuits in larger assemblies;
- the teachers and pupils in a school are the customers of the lab technicians, to whom they provide a service;
- the customers of a payroll clerk are the employees whose wages he or she calculates.

Everyone in the workplace has customers.

Let's look at an example of what the effects can be when internal customers are not satisfied.

Imagine a large corporation with a wide range of services and products. Somewhere tucked away in just one of the corporation's many factories, there is a team part of whose job it is to collect and dispose of the kitchen waste from the factory's several canteens.

Not a very important task, you might say. Certainly not a very visible one, from the point of view of the corporation's external customers. Only employees eat in the canteen, not customers. And the average employee eating his or her lunch doesn't give a moment's thought to the job of clearing away kitchen waste.

Activity 15

3 mins

Who might be the 'customers' of the waste-disposal team?

_____

How can the work that this team does have any possible effect on the prosperity of the organization?

_____

_____

_____

The team's immediate customers might be the kitchen supervisors.

Let's think what might happen if the team does not satisfy their customers.

Suppose they do a less than good job – perhaps waste is left in and around the kitchens for much longer than it should be, for example. There are several possible consequences of the poor quality of their work, including the following.

- Uncollected waste will probably encourage bacteria and vermin, which may in turn endanger the health of the kitchen staff and the employees eating food from the kitchens; in the worst case, the resultant illness and absenteeism could directly affect the corporation's profits.
- The kitchen staff may become accustomed to seeing waste lying about. This could easily make them feel that 'sloppy' standards of work are acceptable. They in turn may do less than their best, and so will probably make **their** customers dissatisfied.
- The kitchen supervisors, struggling to do a good job, may become frustrated with the service they are getting. If nothing is done about the problem, some may even want to leave. If they do, the corporation will need to pay out more for recruitment and training.

You can see that there is a kind of chain reaction taking place:

Poor quality work . . .

. . . leads to . . .

. . . dissatisfied customers and poor quality work . . .

. . . which lead to . . .

. . . dissatisfied customers and poor quality work . . .

. . . which lead to . . .

If the final customer doesn't suffer, the organization certainly will, and so will its employees.

Now let's look on the positive side. The chain works the other way, too. High quality work – whatever it is – nearly always results in:

■ happy and satisfied customers (whether internal or external);
■ the setting of higher standards, which others tend to follow;
■ more satisfied employees – because everyone gets more satisfaction from doing a good job than doing a bad one;
■ a more successful organization.

This idea is shown in the diagram below.

In the Work-based assignment for this workbook, you will be asked to identify your team's internal customers, and to identify ways of improving your service to them.

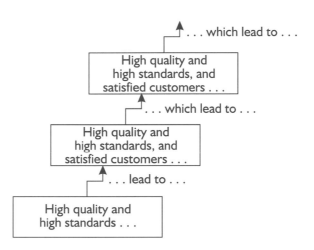

. . . which lead to . . .

High quality and
high standards, and
satisfied customers . . .

. . . which lead to . . .

High quality and
high standards, and
satisfied customers . . .

. . . lead to . . .

High quality and
high standards . . .

6 A commitment to quality

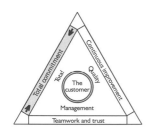

Total quality management, more than anything, demands a **total commitment to quality** on behalf of everyone involved. To achieve the aim of 'continuous improvement towards perfection', the whole organization has to be geared towards quality.

An essential concept of TQM is that

every person and every group is involved in quality.

This means that quality concerns:	not only in:	but also in:
■ all employees ■ all processes ■ all functions ■ all departments and ■ all activities	■ manufacturing ■ service provision ■ service and product design ■ product and service verification ■ procurement	■ marketing ■ sales ■ finance ■ personnel ■ and all other departments, workgroups and functions.

But how do you maintain people's commitment to a quality programme? Many programmes have failed, not because the fundamental ideas were wrong, or because initial enthusiasm was lacking, but that

maintaining a commitment to quality is far more difficult than getting started.

Three essential management tools for maintaining commitment are:

- **consistency**: in other words, meaning what you say, without allowing yourself to lose sight of the overall goals;
- **communications**: saying what you mean, and being willing to share information;
- **involvement**: allowing every member of the team to participate fully.

6.1 Being consistent

> **EXTENSION 3**
> The leadership aspects of quality management are dealt with extensively in *Leadership for Quality*, by Frances Clark. The book is listed on page 76.

When TQM is introduced, it entails a change of attitude and approach on the part of everyone. When people are asked to participate actively in such a programme, they will naturally look to managers for leadership. A certain amount of scepticism can be expected.

Activity 16

What kinds of questions are likely to form in the minds of staff when an initiative such as TQM is introduced? Think about your own team, and the questions they might ask themselves, especially about management's intentions. Jot down two questions.

_____

_____

_____

_____

_____

_____

Typically, as you may agree, people will ask themselves questions such as:

'We hear the words, but does management mean what it says?'

'Who will be rewarded – those who stick to the old rules, or those who try to live up to the new ideals, and inevitably make mistakes?'

'When things get difficult, will management hastily revert to a policy of making the best of things, or will it remain true to the TQM concepts?'

In other words, among other things, staff will look to management for **consistency** in their application of the new system.

6.2 Communicating

To become committed to the TQM cause, and to remain so, people will want lots of information. They will need to:

- be trained in the concepts of TQM, and how they should be applied;
- be reminded at frequent intervals about these concepts;
- be guided in adapting their behaviour;
- have feedback on their performance;
- be told how the customers are reacting to the new approach;
- be informed about progress, locally and in the organization as a whole.

7 Teamwork and trust

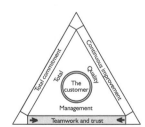

TQM will only work if there is complete commitment, not only by management, but by everyone in the organization. No single person or department can make TQM operate successfully: it needs the full co-operation of all staff and all departments.

That's why teamwork and mutual trust are essential ingredients in the TQM recipe.

We will take up these topics again in the next session, and deal more fully with the 'teamwork and trust' dimension of total quality management.

Self-assessment 2

1 In the following grid, there are eleven words hidden, which are key to the subject of total quality management. (All of them were mentioned in this session.) The words may run forward or backwards, up or down, or diagonally in any direction. See if you can find all eleven.

C	U	S	T	O	M	E	R	O	T
K	O	O	L	P	E	A	K	N	H
R	E	N	T	O	L	L	E	T	G
O	D	O	T	A	Y	M	T	S	I
W	H	E	T	I	E	A	A	U	L
M	S	O	T	G	N	I	L	R	E
A	T	R	A	A	H	U	R	T	D
E	N	N	U	I	I	P	O	L	Y
T	A	N	Y	T	I	L	A	U	Q
M	W	O	N	G	I	S	E	D	S

2 Write down a definition of total quality management.

_____

_____

_____

3 What would you say to someone in your organization who claimed: 'I don't have customers – I just get on with my job, by obeying instructions.'

_____

_____

_____

_____

_____

4 Complete the words and phrases in the following diagram:

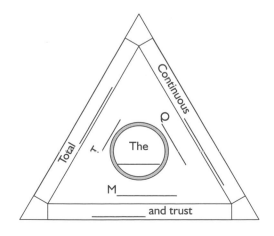

Answers to these questions can be found on pages 80–1.

8 Summary

■ The traditional view of quality management was that it was something that one of the organization's departments did, and that quality problems could be blamed on the quality manager.

■ **Total quality management (TQM)** involves every member of the organization in a process of continuous improvement with the aim of satisfying the customers' wants and expectations.

■ Customers want more than to be satisfied – they want to be **delighted**! In order to 'delight' customers, you have to give them **more** than they expect.

■ There are three key elements to TQM:

  ■ **continuous improvement**;
  ■ **teamwork**, involving **trust** and **empowerment**;
  ■ **focusing on the customer's wants and expectations.**

■ Continuous improvement is often referred to by its Japanese name *kaizen*. It is characterized by:

  ■ a large number of **detailed** improvements,
  ■ over **a long period** of time,
  ■ involving **teams** throughout the organization.

■ Successful commercial organizations recognize that building up **customer loyalty** has to be a key element in their marketing strategy. This can be done by:

  ■ delivering a level of quality that is consistently high;
  ■ putting the wants and expectations of the customer first – for without customers there is no business;
  ■ establishing a culture in which all employees are expected to display a commitment to the customer.

■ Everyone in the workplace has customers. Internal customers are nearly as important as external ones.

■ Three essential management tools for maintaining commitment are:

  ■ **consistency**: meaning what you say, without allowing yourself to lose sight of the overall goals;
  ■ **communications**: saying what you mean, and being willing to share information;
  ■ **involvement**: allowing every member of the team to participate fully.

Session C Practical steps to quality

1 Introduction

'What does "making quality certain" mean? "Getting people to do better all the worthwhile things they ought to be doing anyway" is not a bad definition.'
— **Philip Crosby,** *Quality is Still Free.*

> Philip Crosby recommends a zero defects programme lasting between a year and eighteen months. The last step in his list of recommendations is 'Now do it over again'. (See Extension 2).

There is no simple magic formula for quality. High quality goods and services are not an automatic outcome of any system or routine process. Accreditation to ISO 9000 or any other standard won't guarantee success; rather like passing an exam, it means little more than that you have a certain amount of knowledge and have the potential for doing well. Even total quality management, if it is applied half-heartedly, or without full commitment, will not ensure that your customers will be delighted with your quality.

As we've discussed, quality improvement and development only comes about through total commitment and a great deal of hard work. But 'one big push' won't be enough. You have to keep up the effort and enthusiasm all the time, over and over again.

We've agreed that quality has to be recognized as an organization-wide problem. In this last session, we'll look at some practical steps that team leaders can take, while playing their part in the overall scheme of things. But before we do that, we should compare two different approaches to quality improvement.

2 Finding ways to improve quality

As a first line manager, you will no doubt be expected to comply with the systems that exist within your own organization. Let's just for a moment look at the possible approaches to the development of quality performance that may be adopted.

2.1 Approaches to quality improvement

In the book *The Fundamentals of Quality Management*, Dennis F. Kehoe contrasts the 'innovation approach', often adopted by Western companies, and the 'continuous improvement approach', promoted by the Japanese.

47

We have already discussed continuous improvement, or *kaizen*.

Kaizen is characterized by:

- a large number of **detailed** improvements;
- over **a long period** of time;
- involving **teams** throughout the organization.

The innovation approach involves:

- a few **large-scale** improvements;
- at **infrequent** intervals;
- initiated by **management**.

Which is the right way? Dennis F. Kehoe suggests that:

'In reality the real quality development challenge is not how to choose between improvement- or innovation-based strategies, but how to combine the benefits of both approaches to enhance business performance. Long-term competitive advantage is achieved through the application of both improvement and innovation ... Most companies therefore need to understand and combine both the techniques ...'

That seems reasonable. But to improve the quality of a product or service, it's first necessary to understand what the problems are.

2.2 Do you know where the problem lies?

Surely, it is true to say that most organizations know where their quality problems exist. If you are making a product – such as garden gnomes, electric saws, skin cream, or pet food – or else providing a service – such as hairdressing, personal fitness training, newspaper delivery, or financial consultancy – you would obviously know what quality problems you have. Or would you?

Activity 17

3 mins

Try to think of two reasons why a product or service supplier might **not** be aware of its quality problems.

_____

_____

_____

_____

_____

There are several possible reasons. An organization might not:

■ be aware of its customers' complaints: as we've discussed, most customers don't complain about the problems they experience;

■ have proper systems in place which enable it to identify quality problems;

■ have good internal communication, so that problems identified in one area may not be conveyed to others;

■ be willing to recognize problems when it sees them: for example, how often have you talked to a salesperson about the difficulties you've had, only for it to be suggested that it's you that's at fault, rather than the product?

■ see problems when they exist, but only the symptoms of those problems. If orders are falling, it may be hard to find out why.

So, before it can solve its quality problems, an organization has to be able to identify them. How can this be done?

One way is to make use of the knowledge and skills of the people who are closest to the work, that is, first line managers and their teams. Time and again, it has been shown that those who perform the work – operators, technicians, clerks, warehouse staff, sales assistants and others who function 'at the workface' – are the ones best able to identify quality problems. First line managers are therefore well placed to report, record and (quite often) help the team to rectify these problems. More senior managers must keep the larger picture in mind, and often have insufficient knowledge of the detail to identify quality problems, with little time to learn it.

In recognizing this fact, many organizations have introduced team-based quality improvement programmes.

3 Working as a team

One team-based approach is **quality improvement groups**.

3.1 Quality improvement groups

These became popular in this country in the early 1980s. The term originally used was **quality circles**. The concept – continuous improvement through teamwork – is a basic component of total quality management, and this is only one way that it may be implemented.

Quality improvement groups are also sometimes called **quality action groups**. Their purpose is to encourage active employee participation in solving quality problems.

- A typical quality improvement team is a group of around six people from the same workplace who meet regularly – say around an hour a week. The team leader is often a front line manager.
- People belonging to quality improvement teams are volunteers. There can be no question of instructing people to join.
- The team members decide which problems they will tackle. This is important, because each problem should be one the members have to face in their working lives – ones they are aware of and can get information about.
- They solve their own problems wherever possible. If more resources are needed, the help of others in the organization may be called upon.

It has to be said that implementation of the idea is not without difficulties.

Activity 18

4 mins

From what you know about quality improvement teams, can you think of any reason why they may not work as well as expected? Jot down two reasons, if you can.

Even if you have no direct personal experience of quality improvement teams, you should still be able to make some good guesses in answer to this question, based on what you've learned so far from this workbook. Think for a few minutes about what happens when people sit down together to try to solve problems – especially people who aren't used to doing this kind of thinking. Bear in mind the kind of support they need and the difficulties they face.

_____

_____

_____

_____

_____

_____

The subject of roles in teambuilding is covered in the Super Series 3 workbook *Working in Teams.*

There may be a number of reasons why quality improvement teams do not work as well as expected, including the following:

Difficulty	Comment
The team does not receive enough support or recognition from management: no work group can hope to achieve a great deal if it is being ignored.	This is especially true of people with no experience of group problem solving.
There is insufficient training of team members, which is likely to prevent them being able to get to grips with the problems they are trying to solve.	Training is needed in how to approach the task, how to collect evidence, how to analyse data, how to present results, and so on.
There is poor communication between the circle and management, so that nobody is quite sure what the circle is up to.	As we have already discussed, communication is a key factor in improving quality. It's surprising how often employees will assume that their manager knows everything that goes on!
The team tries to solve problems which they have insufficient information about, and perhaps jump to conclusions rather than taking the time and trouble to find this information.	Sometimes the 'instinctive' or obvious reaction is the most effective. A group may be able to solve some problems without too much effort. It may then assume – mistakenly – that any problem can be solved in this fashion.
Clashes of personality occur within the team, including perhaps some people trying to dominate the discussions, while others are ignored.	This is a difficult one, requiring considerable managerial skills on behalf of the team leader. Volunteer teams do not always attract the ideal mixture of personalities and talents, so that all the required team roles are not covered.
Team members are not given the time to do the necessary work in collecting and analysing data.	It is often wrongly assumed that a 'once a week' session is all that's needed, after which everyone can go back to work. But when the data isn't to hand, someone has to be set to work actively seeking it out.
The team leader is uncommitted, too inexperienced, or simply incompetent.	Training for the leader may be needed, too.
Teams may tackle problems which are too large for them to deal with adequately.	Over-ambition is a common failing.
The team does not have a suitable place to meet.	This is a basic error. It stems from lack of management support.

3.2 How quality improvement teams work

The fundamental idea of quality improvement teams is sound: that of getting employees involved in solving their own quality problems. But making quality improvement teams **work in practice** needs commitment and good management.

The starting point for quality improvement team activities is to identify and select a problem for the team to tackle. Problems may be brought to the attention of the circle in a number of ways, but they should be ones which members can become involved in and get information about.

The team has then to decide on ways of tackling the problem. The technique of **brainstorming** may be used.

The essential steps of a brainstorming session are:
- Members meet in a relaxed atmosphere, away from interruptions.
- The subject is introduced by the leader, and then anyone can make any suggestion, however far-fetched, as a solution to the problem.
- No attempt is made to criticize or analyse the ideas until they've all been written down.

Once the quality improvement team has decided on an approach to a problem, there will probably be a need to collect information about it. Often, one person is given the task of fact-finding and analysis of the problem.

When the member reports back to the circle, the ideas and results are discussed. The solution may already be apparent. If it isn't, the circle may decide to do further work or perhaps to bring in others to help. If a solution **has** been found, it is presented to management for approval.

Clearly, quality improvement teams can form a useful function in an organization's overall quality programme, although only a broad outline of the subject has been given in this section.

There is certainly no harm in getting your team involved in talking about quality and about the problems they face, and we will discuss ways of doing this next.

You may want to bear in mind, however, that a formal quality improvement team shouldn't be set up in isolation. To be fully effective, it needs the full commitment and backing of management. You may think it advisable to discuss the idea with your manager first.

4 Getting your team to work for quality

Quality development and improvement entails:

Many quality techniques are described in another workbook in this series: *Achieving Quality.*

■ **systems**; to remind you, a quality system is defined as:

The organizational structure, responsibilities, procedures, processes and resources for implementing quality management.

■ **techniques**, such as data collection and analysis, and statistical process control, which are very important, although we will not discuss them in this workbook;

■ **people**.

As a manager, you probably won't be surprised to learn that, of these three 'keystones of quality', it is people that are the most difficult to manage, and yet offer the greatest potential for success.

4.1 Meeting quality goals

No matter what quality systems are in place where you work, or which techniques are employed, it will be part of your job to organize your team to achieve its quality goals.

Quality goals can be expressed as simple general catch phrases like: 'Zero defects!' or may be more specific and related to the task. All task-related goals should be: SMART:

> **S**pecific
> **M**easurable
> **A**greed
> **R**ealistic
> **T**ime constrained

Specific goals help the team to focus their activities, by defining exactly what must be achieved. In manufacturing, quality requirements are usually written down: 'Part to be machined to 30.5 mm ± 0.2 mm'; 'Surface to be free of blemishes'; 'All edges to be double-stitched' and so on.

Examples of quality goals in service are: 'No customer is to be kept waiting longer than five minutes'; 'All queries are to be dealt with on the day they are raised'; 'Your aim is to make the customers feel you are happy to be serving them'.

Making goals **measurable** means that there is some way of deciding whether or not, or to what extent, the goal has been reached. For example, there is no point in stating a requirement of 'straight edges' if it is open to debate as to 'how straight is straight?'. And it is not sensible to require delivery within a certain time period if you have no means of knowing when a delivery is late.

Quality goals should ideally be **agreed** – the people who have to reach the goals need to have some say in setting them. More organizations are encouraging teams to set their own goals and make their own decisions.

When goals are agreed, they are more likely to be **realistic**. There's little value in asking people to achieve goals they are not equipped for. For instance, it might seem a good idea to demand of sales staff that they smile all the time, but can anybody actually smile through a whole day's work? As another example, if there is a requirement that all telephone calls be answered before the third ring, then there must be staff waiting to answer those calls.

Goals should also be **time-constrained**. This means that achievements should be assessed at the end of a predetermined period. People need to know how well they are doing; even if the goal is an on-going one. At regular intervals, the team needs to look back and review progress, and to re-evaluate their goals in the light of past performance.

So, in order to achieve quality goals, the team leader has to try to ensure that they are specific, measurable, agreed, realistic and time-constrained. This entails:

- giving specific information to team members, in sufficient detail, and at a level and pace appropriate to the individuals concerned;
- making sure this information is understood;
- monitoring quality of work at appropriate intervals;
- ensuring corrective action is taken when goals are not being reached;
- keeping complete and accurate records, which of course should comply with organizational requirements.

By completing the next activity, you can assess your own performance in helping to achieve quality goals.

| Portfolio of evidence A1.1 | Activity 19 | 15 mins |

This Activity is the first of a series of three which together may provide the basis of appropriate evidence for your S/NVQ portfolio. If you are intending to take this course of action, it might be better to write your answers on separate sheets of paper.

Give an example of a specific quality goal you set your team.

_____

_____

_____

_____

Explain how you measure achievement against this goal.

_____

_____

_____

_____

_____

Do the team have a say in setting this and other goals? If so, explain how they are brought into the discussions. If not, explain what actions you intend to take to help the team set their own goals in future.

_____

_____

_____

_____

_____

Explain how you might improve the way in which you provide information about quality requirements to your team members, at a level and pace appropriate to the individuals concerned.

_____

_____

_____

_____

_____

Explain how you might do more to confirm that each individual understands his or her quality commitments.

_____

_____

_____

_____

_____

Give an example of the action you take when you find that your team's work is not up to standard.

_____

_____

_____

_____

_____

4.2 Work conditions

By 'conditions' we mean the physical environment, equipment, materials, or working procedures.

It is difficult to produce high quality work in poor conditions.

Fairly obviously, work conditions should be healthy and safe – this comes before all other requirements. But setting up and maintaining the right conditions for quality is also part of the first line manager's job.

For some kinds of work, quality and health and safety may go together. If your team is handling food, then you will need to ensure that appropriate levels of hygiene are met consistently. Zero defects in food preparation may include the goal of zero contamination by unhealthy bacteria; to achieve this, the work environment must be kept immaculately clean.

In other jobs, achieving the right work conditions for quality may be a matter of carrying out activities such as checking on the ambient temperature, or insisting that the work area be kept clean and tidy. People will work at less than their full potential if they:

- are too hot or too cold;
- have too little light;
- suffer draughts or noise;
- are expected to work in dirty or cluttered conditions;
- must use inappropriate tools or materials;
- have outdated equipment, incapable of producing work of the required standard;
- get too many interruptions;
- are required to follow instructions or procedures which are incorrect or difficult to follow.

Portfolio of evidence A1.2

Activity 20

15 mins

This Activity may provide the basis of appropriate evidence for your S/NVQ portfolio. If you are intending to take this course of action, it might be better to write your answers on separate sheets of paper.

Give two examples of the kind of information your team members need, in order to meet their responsibilities for maintaining healthy, safe and productive work conditions.

_____

_____

_____

_____

_____

What steps do you plan to take to keep them better informed in this respect?

_____

_____

_____

_____

_____

What kind of training do your team members need to receive to ensure that they will meet quality standards or goals in the conditions which they have to work under?

_____

_____

_____

_____

_____

What steps do you intend to take to ensure this training is appropriate and sufficient?

_____

_____

_____

_____

_____

Explain the steps you have taken, or intend to take, to ensure that team members are given every opportunity to make recommendations for improving work conditions.

_____

_____

_____

_____

_____

Explain how you intend to take actions to improve work conditions, so that they meet the requirements of your organization, comply with the law, and are more conducive to the performance of high quality work.

_____

_____

_____

_____

Provide an example (or a copy of an actual document in your portfolio), of your record-keeping with regard to work conditions, especially any that relate to organizational or legal requirements.

_____

_____

_____

_____

_____

4.3 Recommending improvements to quality-related activities

When you or your team identify a quality problem, you may be in a position to solve it straight away. If you spot a member of your team using the wrong tool, talking to a customer in an inappropriate manner, or failing to follow an agreed procedure, you may be able to take immediate corrective action.

In other cases, perhaps where a whole batch of work is found not to be up to standard, the steps to put it right may take longer, but you may still be able to contain the problem within your own work area.

But sometimes, first line managers don't have the authority and/or the resources to solve quality problems. Where there is a faulty design or process, or a matter which affects other teams, your best course of action may be to make a recommendation to others. You may need to pass your recommendations to:

- colleagues at the same level as yourself;
- higher level managers;
- specialists; or perhaps to
- your team members.

| Portfolio of evidence A1.3 | Activity 21 | 15 mins |

This Activity may provide the basis of appropriate evidence for your S/NVQ portfolio. If you are intending to take this course of action, it might be better to write your answers on separate sheets of paper.

Give an example of a recommendation you have made, or intend to make, regarding improvements to quality.

_____
_____
_____
_____
_____
_____

Explain to what extent your recommendation is consistent with team objectives, and the values and policies of your organization.

_____
_____
_____
_____
_____
_____

List the other parts of the organization that your recommendations will impinge upon, and describe the ways in which each of them will be affected.

_____
_____
_____
_____
_____
_____

Is your recommendation presented in a clear manner, and in a form that is consistent with organizational procedures? Explain, briefly.

_____
_____
_____
_____
_____
_____

4.4 Empowering teams

Of course, you can't be expected to come up with all the ideas. Your team members should be encouraged to make suggestions for quality improvements, too.

Activity 22

What actions can you or do you take to encourage suggestions from your team?

_____

_____

_____

_____

_____

_____

You might:

■ simply ask them for their ideas, either about specific problems, or in general;
■ show appreciation or reward them for good suggestions: some organizations have a graded system of rewards, and each serious idea is formally evaluated;
■ set up some kind of competition.

Perhaps you agree that the best way to get people to do anything is to **motivate** them to do it – to get them in a frame of mind so that they **want** to do it. And you will motivate a team or a group if they feel that they **own** their own work and problems.

What does this concept of ownership mean? It is based on the premise that people are better motivated to work for themselves and something that is theirs, than for other people or other people's ideas.

Many employees are made to feel that they are simply being paid to do a job, and that they are expected to do what they're told, without discussion or argument. Where this is the case, they will, at best, do what is required of them. Typically, they will do the absolute minimum of work that they feel they can get away with.

But if they can be:

- given the opportunity to make many of their own decisions and set their own standards;
- persuaded to take a pride in their work because it is in their own interests to do so; (as we have discussed, these benefits include greater job security, and potentially higher rewards in the longer term).
- shown ways to manage themselves as a team;

then they are much more likely to excel at what they do.

This approach naturally leads to the concept of **empowerment**. One way to describe empowerment is as follows:

EXTENSION 4
This book, listed on page 76, is a useful introduction to the subject of empowerment.

'The empowered workplace stems from a new relationship between employees and a new relationship between people and the organization. They are partners. Everyone not only feels responsible for their jobs, but feels some sense of ownership of the whole. The work team does not just react to demands, it is an initiator of action. The employee is a decision maker, not follower. Everyone feels that they are continually learning and developing new skills to meet new demands.'
— Cynthia D. Scott and Dennis T. Jaffe, *Empowerment*.

A branch of one large organization improved quality and increased productivity by introducing the following steps:

- rooms were added where people in teams could meet;
- communication was improved between shifts, by holding thirty-minute meetings as one shift handed over to the next;
- all types of news was shared with staff – good news and bad;
- self-managed teams of about a dozen people were set up;
- multiskilling was encouraged, and a skill-based pay system set up;
- pay progression depended on the views of peers, not superiors;
- managers were called team leaders;
- everyone wore the same uniform.

Empowerment is not a technique – it is a culture. As such, individual managers or team leaders cannot introduce the concept – it needs the full support of the organization. If you work where empowerment has been introduced, you will no doubt be aware of its benefits. If you don't, you may want to talk over the idea with your colleagues, and find out more about it.

5 Zero defects programmes

The term 'zero defects' was coined by Philip Crosby, when he was a departmental quality manager employed by the Martin-Marietta Corporation in 1962, working on the Pershing missile programme. He writes:

'It was during this time that I developed the concept of zero defects (ZD) because we could just not learn how to find everything that could be wrong in a weapons system. We had to prevent, not sort. . . . Later, when I was managing supplier quality, we were able to help the suppliers get us the right stuff, on time.

Perhaps your own organization has used the ZD slogan, and you may have been involved in implementing a programme based on it. The key to zero defects is in **prevention** of errors, rather than their detection. Every individual and every team must learn never to pass on defective work.

A zero defects programme may entail the following steps.

- **Identifying the organization's quality problems.**
- **Agreeing quality goals**: what is to be achieved, and **setting clear targets** against which progress can be measured.
- Devising means of **motivating people** to believe in the programme. This would almost certainly entail **full employee participation**: empowering teams and team members to 'take ownership' of the programme. The high ideals of zero defects must be introduced by management, and have their full commitment, but it is the employees who must be given the opportunity to make the programme their own. Simply sticking up ZD posters will achieve very little; it's only when people start to talk about it and get enthusiastic about it that the programme will take off.
- **Establishing formal, regular, simple procedures for reporting** achievement of the targets.
- **Organizing jobs** in order to make the programme work.
- **Encouraging a full and free flow of information**.

Self-assessment 3

15 mins

1 Match each term or phrase on the left with **three** of the items listed on the right.

A Continuous improvement

_____

B The innovation approach to quality improvement

_____

C Quality improvement groups

_____

a steps taken at infrequent intervals

b teams of around six people

c volunteers trying to improve quality

d many actions taken over a long period of time

e initiated by management

f people from the same workplace

g involving teams throughout the organization

h a large number of detailed improvements

i large-scale improvements

2 List two difficulties that a quality improvement group might need to overcome.

_____

_____

_____

_____

_____

_____

_____

_____

3   Fill in the blanks in the following sentences with suitable words taken from the list below.

    a Quality development and _____ entails:

       ■ _____: The organizational _____, responsibilities, procedures, processes and _____ for implementing quality management.

       ■ _____, such as data collection and analysis, and statistical process control;

       ■ people.

    b It is difficult to produce high _____ in _____ work conditions.

    c Teams are much more likely to _____ at what they do if they can be:

       ■ given the _____ to make many of their own _____ and set their own _____;

       ■ persuaded to take a _____ in their work because it is in their own _____ to do so;

       ■ shown ways to manage _____ as a team.

DECISIONS	EXCEL	IMPROVEMENT	INTERESTS
OPPORTUNITY	POOR	PRIDE	QUALITY
RESOURCES	STANDARDS	STRUCTURE	SYSTEMS
TECHNIQUES	THEMSELVES		

4   The main aim of old-fashioned quality control was the detection of errors. What is the aim of a 'zero defects' programme?

_____

_____

_____

Answers to these questions can be found on pages 81–2.

6 Summary

- **Continuous improvement** involves a large number of small detailed improvements over a long period and involving teams. The **innovation approach** entails large-scale improvements, introduced by management at infrequent intervals. Both approaches have advantages.

- Organizations are seldom able to identify all their quality problems, for various reasons.

- Often, it is employees at the low end of the hierarchy who are able to identify what the real problems are.

- **Quality improvement groups** may consist of a small team of volunteers, who choose the problems they want to tackle.

- A number of difficulties may be faced by such groups, but these may be overcome through support and training.

- Quality development and improvement entails:

  - **systems**: the organizational structure, responsibilities, procedures, processes and resources for implementing quality management;
  - **techniques**, such as data collection and analysis, and statistical process control;
  - **people**.

- All task-related quality goals should be: SMART:

  Specific
  Measurable
  Agreed
  Realistic
  Time constrained

- People will tend to work at less than their full potential if they suffer from poor quality **work conditions**, i.e. physical environment, materials, equipment, or working procedures.

- Team leaders are often expected to make clearly presented **recommendations** about quality, which are consistent with team objectives and organizational procedures.

- Empowerment means giving teams and individuals the power to make their own work decisions.

- A **zero defects** programme is based on the concept of **prevention**, rather than cure.

Performance checks

1 Quick quiz

Jot down the answers to the following questions on *Understanding Quality*.

Question 1   Which group of people ultimately make all the decisions, and set all the standards, regarding the quality of a product or service?

_____

Question 2   What do we mean by the 'utility' or 'performance' of a product?

_____

_____

_____

Question 3   What kinds of activities are quality control specialists involved in?

_____

_____

_____

Question 4   Explain why quality control can't deliver high quality on its own.

_____

_____

_____

Question 5   What is the driving force which makes organizations want to improve their quality standards?

_____

_____

_____

Question 6   In one sentence, what is meant by prevention costs?

_____

_____

_____

Question 7   What's the difference between internal failure costs and external failure costs?

_____

_____

_____

Question 8   How would you define reliability?

_____

_____

_____

Question 9   Name two potential benefits to an organization of accreditation to ISO 9000.

_____

_____

_____

Question 10   What guarantee does accreditation to ISO 9000 provide that an organization will meet its quality goals?

_____

Question 11   Write down the main concepts involved in total quality management.

_____

_____

_____

Question 12   What exactly do we mean by 'continuous improvement'?

_____

_____

_____

Question 13   Explain what is meant by the statement: 'Everybody in the workplace has customers.'

_____

_____

_____

Question 14   Give two possible reasons why a typical organization is not aware of all its quality problems.

_____

_____

_____

Question 15   What are the two main ways in which the problems facing quality improvement groups can be minimized.

_____

_____

_____

Answers to these questions can be found on pages 82–3.

2 Workbook assessment

60 mins

Read the following case incident and then deal with the questions which follow, writing your answers on a separate sheet of paper.

■   At the Grimchester Hotel, Myrna Leighton is in charge of general house-keeping, which includes cleaning and replacing supplies. Myrna has a team of five, and between them they have to clean thirty-five rooms, plus the dining room, bars, reception, conference hall and leisure facilities.

The job consists of cleaning and dusting all surfaces, making beds and general tidying, putting out fresh towels and replenishing supplies such as toilet rolls, soap and tea and coffee. Myrna reports to the hotel under-manager, who makes a point of inspecting rooms on a random basis to make sure they are up to the hotel's standards.

You do not need to write more than two or three sentences in reply to each of the following questions.

1   Who are Myrna's team's 'customers'? Give a brief reason for your answer.

2   Suggest a way in which the quality of the service that Myrna's team provides could be measured.

3   How would you suggest that Myrna could best convey the quality standards that the hotel demands, to a new member of the team?

4   If the hotel introduced a system of total quality management, how would you expect that to affect Myrna and her team?

5   Suppose the under-manager is not consistent in his inspection visits: sometimes he picks up on the slightest thing, but at other times he ignores things which Myrna knows to be wrong. How might this result in quality problems?

Portfolio
of evidence
A1.3, D1.1,
D1.2

3 Work-based assignment

60
mins

The time guide for this assignment gives you an approximate idea of how long it is likely to take you to write up your findings. You will find you need to spend some additional time gathering information, perhaps talking to colleagues and thinking about the assignment.

Your written response to this assignment may form useful evidence for your S/NVQ portfolio. The assignment is designed to help you to demonstrate your personal competence in:

- the ability to analyse and conceptualize, by showing that you can think clearly and objectively about the past, and to apply your thinking to present and future plans;
- the team-building skills;
- the ability to focus on results;
- the ability to make decisions;
- the commitment to excellence.

What you have to do

1   Write down the names of all your internal customers. (If you only have external customers, go to step 2.)

2   Identify your customers' wants and expectations, in as much detail as you can. Do this by:

- talking with them, if possible, and asking them to say, or (preferably) write down, what they consider their wants and expectations are;
- talking with other relevant people in your organization.

3   Separately, write down what you believe you currently provide to your customers, again in as much detail as possible.

4   Compare the lists from 2 and 3 above, and identify the differences.

5   Now write down a plan of action, so that you can close the gap between what your customers want and what you actually give them. Make a distinction between what you can do yourself, and the actions which you will require help or further authority to instigate.

Write down your plan in the form of a report or a memo to your manager.

Reflect and review

Now that you have completed your work on *Understanding Quality*, let us review our workbook objectives.

■ When you have completed this workbook you will be better able to explain what quality means.

We have seen that quality can mean different things to different people. However, it is possible to define quality by referring to BS 4778 (ISO 8402):

'The totality of features and characteristics of a product or service that bear on its ability to satisfy stated or implied needs.'

Alternatively, we can say that quality is defined by the customer, because it is whatever the customer wants and expects.

Try answering the following questions.

■ What does quality mean exactly, so far as **your** job and **your** team are concerned. Try to summarize it in a brief statement.

_____

_____

_____

■ Looking a little wider, how important would you say that quality was to your organization?

_____

_____

_____

71

Our second objective was as follows.

■ When you have completed this workbook you will be better able to recognize the benefits of quality improvement and development in your work, and appreciate methods of establishing the costs of quality.

Well, what are the benefits? Will improved quality make you richer, give you a more secure job, and improve your chances of personal development? In fact, it may do all of these things. We have seen that the organization and the customers benefit from quality improvements – and so do employees.

We looked at a method of evaluating quality costs by dividing them into prevention, appraisal and failure costs. However costs are analysed, one thing is clear: the cost of achieving competitive levels of quality is lower than the cost of not achieving them.

■ Write down the benefits of quality improvement in your work. Do this in some detail if you can – spend a few minutes on this.

_____

_____

_____

_____

_____

_____

The third objective was:

■ When you have completed this workbook you will be better able to have a good understanding of total quality management.

Total quality management is not very difficult to sum up in a few sentences, but is definitely hard to implement. When we talk about 'total commitment', that's exactly what we mean. To quote Crosby on commitment:

Quality is something that always starts out to be easy. Someone decides that something should be done about it and summons someone. This is the Marshal Wyatt Earp complex . . . For some reason many executives think that when they decide it is time to call in the marshal, their management commitment is all over. Once they find themselves standing on the roof with a real, and loaded, rifle waiting for the real, and genuinely hostile, bad guys to ride in, the true meaning of management commitment begins to reach them. If they do not move to this level of activity, everyone from bad guys to good guys will know they are just fooling around. No one is going to put their neck out for someone who is just fooling around.

Sadly, there are no Wyatt Earps to ride in boldly and face the bad guys – or cure the bad quality: the managers of an organization have to be their own marshals, and put their own necks out first.

The other aspects of TQM: 'focus on the customer', 'continuous improvement' and teamwork, also entail lots of hard work.

- Are you prepared to put your neck out and face up to the quality problems, and to keep facing up to them? (Explain.)

  _____

  _____

  _____

- To what extent do you and your team aim for continuous improvement? (Explain.)

  _____

  _____

  _____

- How hard do you work at getting your quality right? (Be honest.)

  _____

  _____

  _____

The next objective was:

- When you have completed this workbook you will be better able to identify your customers and find ways of improving the quality of the goods and services you provide them.

Customers are the reason for quality systems and development. Without customers, the organization would not exist. Competition drives up quality, because more than one organization has to strive to gain and hold a share of the market. In countries where there is no competition, such as the former Soviet Union, quality levels are usually very low.

If quality goals are reached, so that customers get what they want and expect, customers are satisfied. Should you manage to exceed your goals, and give your customers more than they expect, you may **delight** them, and increase the chances of them coming back for more.

When you complete the Work-based assignment, if you haven't already done so, you will be asked to define your own customers, and to devise ways of closing the gap between what you give them and what they want.

- Explain how you intend to delight your customers.

  _____

  _____

  _____

73

The last objective is:

■ When you have completed this workbook you will be better able to lead your team in taking practical and positive steps towards higher work quality.

Most work activities depend on teamwork, and the team leader has to find ways to motivate the team in order to meet organizational objectives. As Crosby says: 'If it makes so much sense to get the thing done right, then how come the normal way of operating almost everything is to do the wrong thing first and the right thing second?' The answer is that people need to be motivated to do it right first time; if they think nobody cares about quality, then they won't bother. By cultivating a culture which says 'We care about quality – we are proud of **our** quality' the motivation is suddenly there.

Some of the practical and positive steps were discussed in Session C.

■ **What practical and positive steps do you intend to take? List them all.**

_____

_____

_____

_____

_____

_____

_____

2 Action plan

Use this plan to further develop for yourself a course of action you want to take. Make a note in the left-hand column of the issues or problems you want to tackle, and then decide what you intend to do, and make a note in Column 2.

The resources you need might include time, materials, information or money. You may need to negotiate for some of them, but they could be something easily acquired, like half an hour of somebody's time, or a chapter of a book. Put whatever you need in Column 3. No plan means anything without a timescale, so put a realistic target completion date in Column 4.

Finally, describe the outcome you want to achieve as a result of this plan, whether it is for your own benefit or advancement, or a more efficient way of doing things at work.

Desired outcomes

1 Issues

2 Action

3 Resources

4 Target completion

Actual outcomes

3 Extensions

Extension 1

Book   *The Fundamentals of Quality Management*
Author   Dennis F. Kehoe
Publisher   Chapman & Hall, First edition 1996
ISBN   0 412 62690 X

This book covers most aspects of quality, and is an ideal reader for managers wanting to know more about, and to implement, quality management. As stated in the introduction: 'This book has been written to provide both students and industrial managers with a comprehensive description of the tools and techniques of Quality Management and also to provide a framework for understanding Quality Development.'

Extension 2

Book   *Quality is Still Free*
Author   Philip B. Crosby
Publisher   McGraw-Hill, 1996
ISBN   0 07 014532 6

A 'bed-time reading' book on quality that is very thought-provoking. Philip Crosby's earlier book *Quality is Free* 'was the shot heard around the business world. It heralded the Quality Revolution, made "Zero Defects" a household phrase, and launched a movement that gains power to this day.'

Extension 3

Book   *Leadership for Quality: Strategies for Action*
Author   Frances Clark
Publisher   McGraw-Hill, 1996
ISBN   0 07 707828 4

If you are particularly interested in the leadership aspects of quality management, this book may be right for you. It makes good background reading.

Extension 4

Book   *Empowerment*
Authors   Cynthia D. Scott and Dennis T. Jaffe
Publisher   Kogan Page, 1991
ISBN   0 7494 0650 X

This book describes, in simple terms, the concept of empowerment, and what is needed to be done to achieve it.

These extensions can be taken up via your NEBS Management Centre. They will either have them or will arrange that you have access to them. However, it may be more convenient to check out the materials with your personnel or training people at work – they may well give you access. There are other good reasons for approaching your own people; for example, they will become aware of your interest and you can involve them in your development.

76

Extension 5   List of quality system elements referred to in ISO 9001, 9002 and 9003.

Element	Applicable to this standard? (* = Less stringent requirements apply.)		
	ISO 9001	ISO 9002	ISO 9003

4.1 Management responsibility
    4.1.1   Quality policy
    4.1.2   Organization
	YES	YES*	YES*

4.2 Quality system
    4.2.1   General
    4.2.2   Quality system procedures
    4.2.3   Quality planning
	YES	YES	YES*

4.3 Contract review
    4.3.1   General
    4.3.2   Review
    4.3.3   Amendment to a contract
    4.3.4   Records
	YES	YES	YES

4.4 Design control
    4.4.1   General
    4.4.2   Design and development planning
    4.4.3   Organizational and technical interfaces
    4.4.4   Design input
    4.4.5   Design output
    4.4.6   Design review
    4.4.7   Design verification
    4.4.8   Design validation
    4.4.9   Design changes
	YES	NO	NO

4.5 Document and data control
    4.5.1   General
    4.5.2   Document and data approval and issue
    4.5.3   Document and data changes
	YES	YES	YES

4.6 Purchasing
    4.6.1   General
    4.6.2   Evaluation of subcontractors
    4.6.3   Purchasing data
    4.6.4   Verification of purchased product
	YES	YES	NO

4.7 Control of customer-supplied product	YES	YES	YES
4.8 Product identification and traceability	YES	YES	YES*

Element	ISO 9001	ISO 9002	ISO 9003
4.9 Process control	YES	YES	NO

4.10 Inspection and testing
    4.10.1 General
    4.10.2 Receiving inspection and testing
    4.10.3 In-process inspection and testing
    4.10.4 Final inspection and testing
    4.10.5 Inspection and test records
	YES	YES	YES*

4.11 Control of inspection, measuring and test equipment
    4.11.1 General
    4.11.2 Control procedure
	YES	YES	YES

4.12 Inspection and test status	YES	YES	YES

4.13 Control of non-conforming product
    4.13.1 General
    4.13.2 Disposition of non-conforming product
	YES	YES	YES*

4.14 Corrective and preventative action
    4.14.1 General
    4.14.2 Corrective action
    4.14.3 Preventative action
	YES	YES	YES*

4.15 Handling, storage, preservation and delivery
    4.15.1 General
    4.15.2 Handling
    4.15.3 Storage
    4.15.4 Packaging
    4.15.5 Preservation
    4.15.6 Delivery
	YES	YES	YES

4.16 Control of quality records	YES	YES	YES*
4.17 Internal quality audits	YES	YES	YES*
4.18 Training	YES	YES*	YES*
4.19 Servicing	YES	YES	NO

4.20 Statistical techniques
    4.20.1 Identification of need
    4.20.2 Procedures
	YES	YES	YES*

4 Answers to self-assessment questions

Self-assessment 1 on page 28

1 Your definition of quality could have been the 'official' one: 'The totality of features and characteristics of a product or service that bear on its ability to satisfy stated or implied needs.'

Alternatively, you might have said that 'achieving quality means meeting the customer's wants or expectations'.

2

Aesthetics	What a product looks like, and how it feels, sounds, tastes, and smells.
Design quality	The degree to which the specification of the product or service satisfies customers' wants and expectations.
Process quality	The degree to which the product or service, when it is transferred to the customer, conforms to specifications.
Quality assurance (QA)	All those planned and systematic actions necessary to provide adequate confidence that a product or service will satisfy given requirements for quality.
Quality control (QC)	This is concerned with the operational techniques and activities that are used to fulfil requirements for quality.
Reliability	The ability of an item to perform a required function under stated conditions for a stated period of time.

3 The three regions are shown in the diagram:

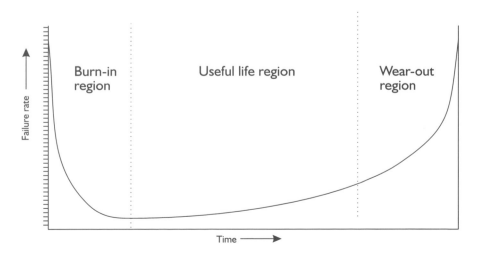

4 The completed table is:

Prevention costs
Appraisal costs } Control costs }
Internal failure costs
External failure costs } Failure costs } Total quality costs

5 a The main driving force behind quality is COMPETITION.
   b The CUSTOMER is the focus of all discussions about quality.
   c DESIGN quality can be defined as the degree to which the SPECIFICATION of the product or service satisfies customers' wants and expectations.
   d PROCESS quality is the DEGREE to which the product or service, when it is transferred to the customer, conforms to specifications.
   e A quality SYSTEM can be defined as the organizational STRUCTURE, responsibilities, PROCEDURES, processes and resources for implementing quality management.
   f Quality is measured by the price of NONCONFORMANCE.
   g Reliability is the ABILITY of an item to perform a required FUNCTION under stated conditions for a stated period of time.

Self-assessment 2 on page 44

1 The grid contained the following words:

CUSTOMER
TOTAL
QUALITY
MANAGEMENT
TEAMWORK
TRUST
CONTINUOUS
WANTS
DELIGHT
DETAIL
LOYALTY

2 Total quality management can be defined in terms of the three words in the name:

■ **total**, because it requires complete and unqualified **commitment** on behalf of everybody in the organization;
■ **quality**, which, as we agreed in our definition, means meeting the wants and expectations of customers;
■ **management**, led from the top.

Key concepts, central to TQM are:

■ **continuous improvement**;
■ **teamwork**, involving **trust** and **empowerment**;
■ **focusing on the customer's wants and expectations**.

3　You might say something like: 'The simple truth is that everyone has customers. You could even consider your boss as your customer, because he or she is the one you aim to please. Who is the next person or group who use your goods or services? They're your customer. If you don't give them what they want and expect, will you keep your job?'

4　The completed diagram is:

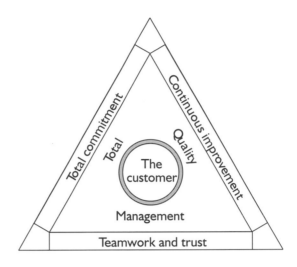

Self-assessment 3 on page 63

1　The correct matches are as follows.

A. Continuous improvement	h a large number of detailed improvements
	d many actions taken over a long period of time
	g involving teams throughout the organization;
B The innovation approach to quality improvement	i large-scale improvements
	a steps taken at infrequent intervals
	e initiated by management
C Quality improvement groups	b teams of around six people
	f people from the same workplace
	c volunteers trying to improve quality.

2　You might want to look back to page 51 for a full answer to this question. In summary, we can say that quality improvement groups will face difficulties without the full support of management. Other difficulties may arise through: lack of training; poor communications; over-ambition; personality clashes; lack of time, a poor team leader; problems that are too big; nowhere suitable to meet.

3 a Quality development and IMPROVEMENT entails:

■ SYSTEMS: The organizational STRUCTURE, responsibilities, procedures, processes and RESOURCES for implementing quality management.
■ TECHNIQUES, such as data collection and analysis, and statistical process control;
■ people.

b It is difficult to produce high QUALITY in POOR work conditions.

c Teams are much more likely to EXCEL at what they do if they can be:

■ given the OPPORTUNITY to make many of their own DECISIONS and set their own STANDARDS;
■ persuaded to take a PRIDE in their work because it is in their own INTERESTS to do so;
■ shown ways to manage THEMSELVES as a team.

4 Put simply, the answer is: 'the *prevention* of errors'.

5 Answers to the quick quiz

Answer 1   There's only one answer: the customers!

Answer 2   We defined utility or performance as the main characteristics of a product or service. It determines what a product does and how well it does it, and what a service provides, and how well it provides it.

Answer 3   Typically, quality control specialists will be involved in:

■ inspection and testing of materials, parts, assemblies and final products, to see whether they conform to defined standards and specifications;
■ using charts and basic statistics to check results and feed back data;
■ maintaining and validating test equipment;
■ sampling services to see whether they meet desired quality levels.

Answer 4   Effective quality must be based on prevention, not detection.

Answer 5   A suitable one-word answer is: competition.

Answer 6   Prevention costs are the costs of setting up a quality management system.

Answer 7   Internal failure costs are those associated with defects detected before the product or service is delivered to the customer; external failure costs occur later.

Answer 8   The 'official' definition is: 'The ability of an item to perform a required function under stated conditions for a stated period of time.'

Answer 9   You might have mentioned: increased levels of business; usually no need for an organization's quality system to undergo investigation by any customer, to any other standard; buying from accredited suppliers gives the customer an assurance that the required level of quality of product or service will be reached; ISO 9000 provides a foundation upon which to build future quality improvements; many larger customers demand ISO 9000/BS 5750 accreditation of suppliers before they will award contracts.

Answer 10   None!

Answer 11   The main concepts of TQM are: total commitment; continuous improvement; teamwork and trust; a focus on the customer's wants and expectations.

Answer 12   Continuous improvement is often referred to by its Japanese name *kaizen*. It is characterized by:

- a large number of **detailed** improvements,
- over **a long period** of time,
- involving **teams** throughout the organization.

Answer 13   Customers can be external or internal. Your customer is the person or group you provide a product or service to.

Answer 14   As we discussed, there are several possible reasons. An organization might not:

- be aware of its customers' complaints: as we've discussed, most customers do not complain about the problems they experience;
- have proper systems in place which enable it to identify quality problems;
- have good internal communication, so that problems identified in one area may not be conveyed to others;
- be willing to recognize problems when it sees them: for example, how often have you talked to a salesperson about the difficulties you've had, only for it to be suggested that it's you that's at fault, rather than the product?
- see problems when they exist, but only the symptoms of those problems. If orders are falling, it may be hard to find out why.

Answer 15   The simple answer to this question is: 'support and training'.

6 Certificate

Completion of this certificate by an authorized person shows that you have worked through all the parts of this workbook and satisfactorily completed the assessments. The certificate provides a record of what you have done that may be used for exemptions or as evidence of prior learning against other nationally certificated qualifications.

Pergamon Flexible Learning and NEBS Management are always keen to refine and improve their products. One of the key sources of information to help this process are people who have just used the product. If you have any information or views, good or bad, please pass these on.

N E B S
M A N A G E M E N T
D E V E L O P M E N T

SUPER S E R I E S

T H I R D   E D I T I O N

Understanding Quality

....

has satisfactorily completed this workbook

Name of signatory   ....

Position   ....

Signature   ....

Date   ....

Official stamp

SUPER SERIES

To Order - phone us direct for prices and availability details
(please quote ISBNs when ordering)
College orders: 01865 314333 • Account holders: 01865 314301
Individual purchases: 01865 314627 (please have credit card details ready)

We Need Your Views

We really need your views in order to make the Super Series 3 (SS3) an even better learning tool for you. Please take time out to complete and return this questionnaire to Marketing Department, Pergamon Flexible Learning, Linacre House, Jordan Hill, Oxford, OX2 8DP.

Name:..

Address:...

....

Title of workbook:..

If applicable, please state which qualification you are studying for. If not, please describe what study you are undertaking, and with which organisation or college:

....

Please grade the following out of 10 (10 being extremely good, 0 being extremely poor):

Content .... Appropriateness to your position ....

Readability .... Qualification coverage ....

What did you particularly like about this workbook?

....
....
....

Are there any features you disliked about this workbook? Please identify them.

....
....
....

Are there any errors we have missed? If so, please state page number: ....

How are you using the material? For example, as an open learning course, as a reference resource, as a training resource etc.

....

How did you hear about Super Series 3?:

Word of mouth: ☐   Through my tutor/trainer: ☐   Mailshot: ☐

Other (please give details):...

....

Many thanks for your help in returning this form.